Please Underestimate Me

Peggy

Never Fear
Never Quit

Please Underestimate Me

The Blood, Guts, and Soul of Richard G. Tripp

Richard G. Tripp

iUniverse, Inc.
New York Lincoln Shanghai

Please Underestimate Me
The Blood, Guts, and Soul of Richard G. Tripp

iUniverse books may be ordered through booksellers or by contacting:

iUniverse
2021 Pine Lake Road, Suite 100
Lincoln, NE 68512
www.iuniverse.com
1-800-Authors (1-800-288-4677)

ISBN: 978-0-595-44210-2 (pbk)
ISBN: 978-0-595-68792-3 (cloth)
ISBN: 978-0-595-88541-1 (ebk)

Printed in the United States of America

Contents

Acknowledgments vii
Preface ix
Introduction xi
Doctor, Am I Going to Die? 1
Visions from My Past 4
He's Just Going to Die 6
Dick, You Had Better Get This Cripple out of This Car 31
My Worst Fears Realized 38
Taxi Time 45
You Can't Leave Me with These Taxi Drivers 49
How Many Mistakes Can One Man Make? 55
Rehabilitation 68
Something Is Coming 73
Waiting Game 79
Flat on My Face My Education in Homelessness Begins 83
Going Backward 86
The Homeless Shelter—One Man's Hope, Another Man's Hell 90
Enough Is Enough 94
Reporting the Truth 98

Shelter Skelter 101
Retribution 104
Dog, St. Louis, and Two Feathers 108
The Real Deal 111
Information Center Indeed 115
Not a Dumb Cab Driver 118
Response 122
Christmas for Everyone 124
Aftermath 127
Not Ready to Make Nice. 130
Devising a Plan 133
Some Kind of Cop. 136
Learning the Ropes 140
Building Bridges 143
Doing My Own Thing 149
Spring Break for the Homeless. 152
Most Underestimate How Far I Will Go to Make a Difference 155
COPP Shops 160
The Teacher's Impact on My Life 164
Helpers along the Way. 168
The Price I've Paid. 173
Where I Stand Today and What Are My Hopes for Tomorrow. 181
Epilogue 183

Acknowledgments

We all have friends who have been there for us in our time of need. We may not see them for years, but they're always there when we need them. Such is the case with Rose (Wood) Boykin. As a young man in the '60s, I got involved in the Job Corps program and was sent to Rodman Job Corps Center in New Bedford, Massachusetts. While there, I went to a coffeehouse run by a church where kids could listen to music and dance and meet other kids. Rose and I met at this coffeehouse and became good friends. As a matter of fact, I ended up taking her to her junior prom. When the time came for me to leave New Bedford and return to Kansas City, we lost touch. In January of 2007, thanks to the Internet, Rose and I reconnected.

This book could not have been completed without the countless hours she put into helping me prepare it for publication. For her help, I'd like to thank her from the bottom of my heart.

Richard G. Tripp

Preface

"But you're not a best-selling author, Richard."

Those words, though true, cut like a knife. They especially hurt because they came from America's number one master of possibilities, Mark Victor Hansen. In the area of human potential, no one is better known or more respected than Mark Victor Hansen. For almost three decades, Mark has helped people and organizations reshape their visions of what is possible. His inspiring motivational messages open his audience members' eyes to realms of possibilities, showing them opportunities for growing, and giving them the resources to act in ways that will change their lives. He has created positive change in thousands of organizations and millions of individuals worldwide.

I attended his "MEGA Marketing Magic" seminar in Los Angeles in 2005. Attending the seminar had been a chance for me to pitch my agenda to some of America's top motivational and networking media gurus and to draw in and find new business associates to help support my work. Following the seminar, as I sat in front of my hotel waiting to catch the airport shuttle, I thought about what my next move should be, and I did a lot of soul searching. Memories of the past and hopes for the future were running around in my head.

I thought back to fourteen years ago, when I had started Care of Poor People, Inc. (COPP), and my motivation for the project then and now. Most who knew me back then would have never thought of me as a crusader for America's poor and homeless brothers and sisters. Those same people definitely wouldn't have thought I could evolve from a man drinking coffee out of a tin can and living under a plastic tarp down by the Missouri River into the new me—a man having coffee in one of America's plushest hotels. People wouldn't believe that the guy waiting for the airport shuttle in the three-piece suit was the same guy who had once worn pants and shirts that were dirty, smelly, and torn. They couldn't know that I had learned to keep dogs with me in the winter time so I could use their body heat to keep me warm during the freezing nights I spent in the hut I'd made from old wooden skids and torn-up plastic sheets truckers used to wrap their tractor trailer loads with at the city market. I was the same guy who used to eat out of dumpsters and who learned to put bread wrappers between his socks and shoes to keep his feet from getting wet and cold. I had learned to survive with basically nothing. Yet just one day prior to this reminiscing, I had addressed seventy millionaires and one billionaire on how they could help America's poor and homeless population.

As I sit in my combination office/bedroom writing this book, I hope to take you back to where I started and the events that propelled me into taking on the mission I am now involved in. I also hope to give you a glimpse of my vision of the future and that you take away from this book an understanding of what you can do to aid those who are hurting.

It is also my desire that you understand the importance of four little words taught to me by one of my mentors, Joe Tye. Those words are "Never Fear, Never Quit," and they can change a person's life. Joe is known as America's Values Coach. He has taught value-based life and leadership skills training, and coaching to corporate and association clients around the globe, and he has been a friend and personal mentor to me for the past ten years. As I stood their speaking to Mark about possibly speaking for free at his next book writing seminar, and telling him about an idea I had for a new book, he listened intensely and then replied, "Well Richard, I'm sure you have what it takes to do both, but I can't just put you on stage without you proving yourself. I know in my being you're capable of both speaking and writing a number one book, and I encourage you to go home and write that number one book, then we will talk about me putting you on stage at my next event"

As our conversation was ending the airport shuttle arrived and I said my farewells to Mark and got on the shuttle. As I left, I had the impression in my mind that Mark might have thought I had just been blowing smoke talking about writing a number one book, and I sort of had the felling that he just might be underestimating my abilities like so many other have throughout my lifetime. But, although I respected him as a teacher I was determined to show him that I would make my dream of a number one book a reality, and prove to him and everyone else, that I was a person not to be underestimated. For I knew the secret word that always propels me ahead when someone doesn't believe in my abilities; the word that keeps me going when things look the worst; the word that holds a powerful meaning for me; one that I learned from the master motivator, Mark Victor Hansen, himself that word is "Next."

Introduction

While this book tells a lot about my personal life, it is my hope that its contents open your eyes to a much bigger problem, a problem that affects many lives. I hope to take you into a world you wouldn't ordinarily travel; I hope to show you the problems faced by America's poor and homeless population; and I hope to show you how your actions might change their lives.

In today's hustle and bustle, we are so tied up in our own little worlds that we don't usually take time to worry about the people living on the streets and their problems. I know in my own life, before I became homeless, I would drive down the street, see them, and take it for granted that if they wanted off the street, all they had to do was get a job. I would rationalize their situation to myself. There were programs set up for these people, weren't there? A lot of my friends, family members, and myself had donated stuff and written checks to various shelters and other organizations. So, I was doing my part for my community, wasn't I? I had my own worries; I didn't need theirs. And besides, I'd written that check to that shelter; that should have taken care of their problems.

Of course, there were special times like Thanksgiving or Christmas when I would go down to a shelter or soup kitchen to serve a meal. This made me feel better about myself, and I could tell my friends what a good Christian I was. Of course, just about any other time of the year I would have just driven by these same people; I'd have never stopped to talk to them. Their world and my world were very different. I worked for everything I got. Besides that, I always wondered if they might have some kind of mental problem or a disease like tuberculosis that I might catch just being near them. It was easier to just write a check, forget about them, and let the soup kitchens and shelters worry about taking care of these folks. At that time in my life, nothing could have prepared me for the lessons I was about to learn.

Today I tell people that homelessness is big business. In America, tens of millions of dollars are spent yearly to help those who are down and out. But instead of these people getting the help they need, the money just disappears. By becoming personally involved in projects to help the poor and homeless in your community, you just might be able to make a difference and give those who are hurting the knowledge that someone does care about them and their welfare, and you might give them a reason to have hope.

Doctor, Am I Going to Die?

It was the second weekend of January 1992. I had rented a motel room that Friday night as a reward to myself and to let off some steam. A couple of weeks earlier, I had hosted the Third Annual Christmas Breakfast for the Homeless, an event I'd started in 1990. The breakfast feeds the homeless in Kansas City, people who otherwise would be put out of the shelters on Christmas morning. The event had been a success, so I figured I had earned this weekend. I was going to just sit back, relax, have some drinks, and chill out. After all, there wasn't anything I really had to do. My taxi fees were paid up for the upcoming week, and it wasn't like I had a wife or kids to worry about. All my kids were grown.

In those days, when I wasn't putting on some event to help the homeless, I often rented a room and got drunk. That was how I relaxed. Prior to 1992, the only time I hadn't been a drinker had been 1990, the year I had been homeless. But as soon as I had gotten back on my feet, as soon as I had started making money in my taxi again, I had returned to the drinking habit that had been with me most of my life. As a homeless man, I just couldn't afford the booze, but those days were over.

I turned on the hotel's television and started mixing myself drinks. I have no idea how many I'd consumed before I passed out. I came to on the floor of the hotel room having no idea what time it was. All I knew was that I was sick as hell, and I felt like I had been run over by a freight train. I was groggy, sick to my stomach, and wondering, "How in the hell did I get on this floor?"

The television was blasting. I heard the announcer say it was Monday morning. I made a couple of feeble attempts at getting up before finally pulling myself across the floor, grabbing onto the bed, and pulling myself up. Sitting there on the nightstand was the bottle of booze I had bought Friday night. I opened it and took a little drink. On Friday night it had been a half-gallon of Canadian Mist whiskey, but now there wasn't much left. However, I didn't have time to give that much thought as I immediately started to gag and throw up.

My initial thought was that the little morning nip I'd just taken had caused me to throw up. Then I saw that there was blood in my vomit. I picked up the phone, called Truman Hospital, and spoke to a nurse. I told her that I'd seen a little blood in my vomit. She said it probably wasn't anything to worry about, but that I should come to the hospital and get checked out.

I hung up the phone, stumbled over to the sink, and got a glass of cold water. I thought the water would make me feel better, but as soon as it hit my stomach I started vomiting blood. There was a lot of blood this time, and it just wouldn't stop. I don't know if I was motivated by panic, shock, or something else, but I knew I had to get to the hospital. I also knew that I didn't have time to wait for help.

I grabbed my car keys, ran out the door, hopped into my taxi, and started for the hospital. I have since been told by the doctors that there is no possible way I could have driven those twenty miles while vomiting the amount of blood I was. But I assure you, that's what I did. On the way to the hospital, I crossed paths with more than one police officer. I tried to get their attention, but I went unnoticed. I ended up driving myself to the hospital that day, but I can assure you there was a guardian angel riding with me.

Upon my arrival at the ER, I made my way to the reception desk and told the nurse seated there that I needed to see a doctor. She looked up from the chart she was holding without looking straight at me, and she started to tell me about the papers I was going to need to fill out. About that time, she looked directly at me and saw that I was covered in blood. I started vomiting again as she yelled for someone to bring a stretcher. I don't know what it was—the loss of blood or relief at knowing that I was going to get some help—but as soon as she'd called for the stretcher, I dropped to the floor.

The attendants picked me up, rushed me back to the ER, hooked me up to all sorts of monitors, and started an IV. The worst part came when they tried to insert a tube into my nose to pump my stomach. After a couple of tries, with me continuously pulling the tube out, they finally tied my hands down.

I was in shock, and a lot of things were running through my mind: How did this happen, and what caused it? Were my friends and family right when they'd told me that my drinking was going kill me someday? I'm only forty three. Don't I have to be older for something like this to happen to me? Did the booze cause this? Am I going to die? What will happen to all the work I've done for the poor and homeless? Hey, God, this can't be happening.

About this time, I looked up into a set of blue eyes. They were the eyes of the female doctor who had run the tube into my nose. She was trying to assure me that I was going to be okay, but at the same time I could see concern in her eyes. I remember asking her if she had gotten a hold of my mother and father. She told me that they were on their way, along with my sister. To this day, I can't get over how blue her eyes were.

I then asked her, "Doctor, am I going die?" She looked down at me and said, "Mr. Tripp, not if we can get the bleeding to stop." Those were the last words I heard her say before I passed out.

Visions from My Past

My mother and father later told me that I'd been put into a drug-induced coma so I could be tended to. I was continuously receiving blood. Before the night was over, I'd lost and been given the equivalent of all my body's blood several times and the hospital's physicians did not expect me to live. As a matter of fact, the woman doctor that examined me in the emergency room, Doctor Fisher, only gave me a 5 percent chance of survival and advised my parents to make funeral arrangements as a precaution. Besides the blood loss, my liver was shot. Doctor Fisher and the other medical specialists in the emergency room thought that my kidneys could fail at any time. I was having trouble breathing. I had to be put on a respirator; and a tracheotomy tube was inserted to help me breathe.

While I was in the coma, I remember going back in time and reliving my life from the time I was a baby in a crib. I remembered my grandmother giving me a toy top while I was in the hospital suffering from polio at age three or four. I remembered almost drowning in a farm pond when I was about five years old. And I remembered my school days and friends I hadn't seen in years.

After reliving the earlier parts of my life, I began to relive my homeless days. I revisited the events that led to my homelessness and the reasons I'd done the things I'd done. I remembered seeing people be abused by the very system that was supposed to help them. I remembered the effect it had on me to be put out in the cold on Christmas morning with other men, women, and, heartbreakingly, children. And I remembered thinking to myself that there must be a better way.

I remembered the little Jewish boy who changed my attitude about the poor and homeless brothers and sisters across our land. At the time, I was living under the Broadway Bridge in Kansas City, Missouri. It was winter, and I had decided that I needed to get in out of the cold. The only way I knew how to do that was to get involved with one of the shelters. So that's what I did. I became a staff member at the Restart shelter. In return, they didn't kick me out at five in the morning. I must tell you, it wasn't for love of my brother or sister that I got involved. I simply got involved so I wouldn't be cold.

However, God decided to show me a lesson through this child. The boy's father owned a sandwich company and routinely brought day-old sandwiches to the shelter to feed the homeless. One day I was in the basement putting the sandwiches away when the little boy approached me and said, "This is for the homeless, too, sir." I took the paper sack he was holding out, stuck it in my pocket, and thanked the little one. I didn't think about it again until later that day when a group of ministry students came to the shelter.

The group was supposed to learn about how the shelter operated, but the guy in charge of the presentation got sick. Although I'd never given a speech in my life, the staff decided I should do it. When I got up on the platform and looked out at the students, I froze. I couldn't speak, but for some reason I remembered that sack in my pocket, and I pulled it out. As I looked into the sack, I felt like a convicted thief, and I started to cry.

What that little boy had given me that day was the contents of his piggy bank. I couldn't help but think, "If a little boy of five could give his change, how much more did Jesus expect me to do?" That's the day I started helping my brothers and sisters, and I haven't stopped since.

I experienced numerous other visions or hallucinations while I was in that coma. To this day I don't know if they were due to the drugs I'd been given or if God was simply showing me things. You see, I not only had visions of my past, but I talked to people who were dead. I talked to a number of departed homeless brothers and sisters I'd been friends with when I too was homeless starting in 1989.

He's Just Going to Die

I continued to relive my life. I watched the good, the bad, and the ugly experiences.

I saw my father bouncing me on his boots when I was a small infant. That had to be back about 1954. I wasn't on his knee like most kids. He would lift his whole foot and hang onto me at the same time; it was like a pony ride. To this day I remember how he was dressed—black motorcycle jacket, black chauffeur hat, and black motorcycle boots with a chrome buckle ring on the side. I remember the piece of white tape he used to cover a mole on the side of his face; he was constantly nicking that mole when he shaved. But the thing I remember feeling above all else was how safe I felt when my father was near. If you've seen *On the Waterfront* with Marlin Brando, then you've seen how my father dressed when I was a child.

I next remembered being pulled out of the farm pond when I was about five years old. By that time, my mother and father had divorced. During the week, my mother worked at a restaurant in Kansas City and boarded my brother, sister, and myself to a couple that lived in the country. This means she paid a couple to baby-sit us during the week while she worked in Kansas City. On that particular day, I snuck out of the farm house and ended up down by the pond. I was playing and somehow fell in. The couple noticed me missing and sent their sixteen-year-old grandson out to look for me. He just happened to spot me at the same time I fell into the pond. He rushed down, jumped in, and saved me. Later that week, after learning of my near-death experience, my mom moved us back to Kansas City with her.

In the next scene, I saw myself when I was 15, wearing my ROTC uniform at Southeast High School on the day President Kennedy was shot. Sitting there in class with my M1 .30 caliber rifle, I wished I had been there to help my president. I will never forget the look on the face of every person in that room when the announcement was made on the school intercom that our president had passed away. Some people cried; others appeared to be ready to go to war. As for myself,

I sat there gripping that M1 rifle. I was more than ready to go to war against whoever was responsible for killing my president.

As the scene switched again, I saw myself as a teenager meeting my first love, Becky. She looked as she had the first time we'd met when I was 15 and she was 14. I then watched as time moved forward and we stood in front of the minister reciting our vows on our wedding day. I was 17 and she was 16 the day we snuck off and got married. Being underage at the time, we were scared that the minister would find out we weren't old enough to be saying those vows. The only way we had been able to get the marriage license issued was because I paid a couple of people to say they were our parents when we went to get our blood test and our license. Becky was still in school, ninth grade if I remember right. Anyway we had to wait three days to get the marriage license issued from the courthouse so we could go get married. That gave us time to make all the plans we would need to get married. We both knew that if our parents knew they would try and stop us from getting married so we planned the whole event out ahead of time. We were smart enough to know if we got caught our parents might try to have the marriage annulled because of our age. What we did was decide to get married out of town and live out of town for at least a month before we let them know where we were. We decided to get married in a little town where nobody really knew us in. That town was Osceola, Missouri. It was a hundred or so miles from Kansas City and we didn't think they would look for us there. During those three days we were waiting for the marriage license, I was busy setting up the hotel room, the bus tickets, and all the other details it would take for us to get married. The year before I had been in Job Corps and graduated from Rodman Job Corps Center in New Bedford, Massachusetts. Upon graduation I had been given a government allotment of 2,000 dollars for the time I had spent in Job Corps. That's the money we used to set up our plans for our marriage. Friday afternoon I picked up the license from the courthouse and then I went to her school to pick her up, and a few hours later we were getting off the bus and going to our hotel room in Osceola, Missouri. The next morning we were at the minister's office getting married there in Osceola. I remember that the old grandfather clock he had in his hallway of his house went tick-tock throughout the ceremony. It was as if our heartbeats were keeping time with the tick-tock of the clock.

Time fast-forwarded again, to when I was 20, and I first saw my baby girl. I remember sitting in the waiting room when the doctor came out and said, "Mr. Tripp, you have a beautiful girl." I was sad because I had wanted a boy, but the minute they brought her out, and she opened her eyes, I was in love. Little did I know at the time, but just a short few months later, I would make one of the biggest mistakes of my life. Because of my actions, I almost missed seeing my baby girl grow up. I remember that night well. I was in a car wreck and almost lost my life. The experience changed me.

The Accident That Changed My Life

Six months prior to the night of the accident, Becky was pregnant with my child for the second time, and things had not been going very well. For one, Becky had stopped wanting to have sex almost as soon as she found out she was pregnant. Maybe it had something to do with the fact that she had miscarried our first baby during the second month of that pregnancy. However, the miscarriage didn't have anything to do with us having sex. And while I tried to understand, the truth was that I couldn't comprehend why the pregnancy was interfering with our love life. I realize that that statement might make me sound like a terrible person, but Becky became colder and less affectionate as the pregnancy progressed, and it seemed that we were drifting farther and farther apart.

One day a friend of mine, Eddie, stopped by my apartment. I told him about the problems Becky and I had been having for the past several months. I'll admit that most men don't share their marital problems with their friends, but Eddie and I had run around together for years, so I trusted him. I confided in him some of the problems I was having with Becky, especially the problems we were having with our sexual relationship.

He said, "Well, Tripp, that's easy enough to fix."

"Oh really, how?"

"Go out and get laid."

"Are you crazy, Eddie? If Becky found out, she would kill me."

"How's she going to find out? You going to tell her, Tripp?" He looked at me with a smirk on his face; it was almost as if he was laughing at me.

"Well, no, but what if somebody saw me or something and it got back to her? What could I tell her? Besides that, Eddie, where would I take another girl where no one would know me?"

"Well, I could rent a motel room out on Highway 40 in my name for a night if you want, Tripp."

"I don't know, Eddie. It would be taking an awfully big chance."

"Well, I've got to go, Tripp. You think about it and let me know."

"Okay Eddie, I'll see you this weekend."

At that time in my life, I was working unloading and loading candy and cigarettes at a warehouse called the Central Candy and Tobacco Company over on the Kansas side of the Missouri river. Back in those days, my health was still good enough for me to do that kind of physical labor. It wasn't a glamorous job, but it paid the rent.

All that next week, I toyed with Eddie's idea. I had run the pros and cons of having an affair through my mind over and over. When Eddie showed up at my apartment complex on Saturday to play a little basketball, I told him that I had been giving the idea some thought, but there were a couple of problems.

"What are the problems, Tripp?" he asked.

"Well, the first problem is that I would have to wait until Becky went out of town for a day or two to see her grandmother or something, like she's doing next week. The second problem is that I don't know any girls."

"You take care of the first problem, Tripp, and I'll set you up with a girl. I know a few."

"Well, Eddie, I wouldn't want a dog, you know," I replied as I only half laughed.

"Don't worry, Tripp. I know a girl that me and the guys have been messing with, and she's just turning eighteen."

"Okay, Eddie, set me up for next week, but if she's a dog, I'll kick your ass, my friend. By the way, what's her name?"

"Debby," was his reply.

The week went by fast, and before I knew it, Friday had rolled around. I got my paycheck and went home. Becky was packed. Becky's mother, Mary, and her boyfriend, Mike, were there waiting to give Becky a ride to her Grandmother's Smith's house for the weekend. Becky gave me a kiss and said, "I'll see you Sunday night, honey."

I said, "Okay," and waved as the trio set off. As I went upstairs to call Eddie, I contemplated backing out of what I had planned. I guess you could attribute my reservations to guilt for what I was about to do. At the same time, I tried to rationalize my actions. The odds were that Becky would never find out about the fling. Besides, I had decided that it was her fault that I had to look for sex elsewhere, because she wasn't providing it at home. At least that's what I was telling myself as I dialed Eddie's phone number. It was easy to blame my actions on someone else and not face the truth about what I was about to do. But there is a name for it—adultery.

Eddie answered the phone.

"Hey, Eddie, it's me. Did you get everything set up for tomorrow?"

"I talked to Debby today, Tripp. She says she'll go out with you, but she wants to talk to you on the phone to see what you're like first."

"You didn't tell her I was married, did you?"

"Hell no, Tripp. I told her that you're just a good friend who lives out of town, and I told her that you'd only be in town for a couple of days."

"Okay, Eddie, I'll take it from here. What's her number?"

He gave me the number.

"By the way, what did you tell her my name is?" I asked.

"Gary. You're Gary Carpenter."

"Good deal," I replied.

Gary Carpenter had been a kid I'd befriended in high school. He'd died from some type of cancer a year or two earlier. On occasion, throughout the years, I used his name as an alias.

"Okay, Eddie, I'll let you go, and I'll give her a call."

I made the connection with Debby that night. The next day, Eddie and his girlfriend picked me up, and we headed over to pick up Debby. Talking to Debby on the phone had been okay, so I thought, "Why not?" At the same time, I had no idea what she looked like, not that it would've really mattered much, as long as she wasn't completely ugly. When we arrived at her house, she came out to the car to meet us. At first sight, I was not impressed by what I saw. Debby had long, brown hair that looked as if it hadn't been brushed in about a million years. Outside of that, she wasn't too bad to look at. As she approached the car, she said that her plans had changed and she could only be gone from home for a couple of hours. Her mother had a doctor's appointment, and Debby had to baby-sit. That messed up what I had planned because I'd been planning to go to a motel.

I looked over at Eddie and said, "Your parents are gone, aren't they?"

"Yep."

"Why don't we go over to your place and have a party?"

"Sounds good to me," he replied.

Debby returned to the house, got her coat, told her mother we wouldn't be gone very long, and promised that she would be back in time to baby-sit. We left and headed over to Eddie's parents' place.

What can I say? Within an hour I had her undressed, and by the time the next hour rolled around we were pulling up to her mother's house and saying our good-byes. I had finally gotten some sexual relief, but now the guilt was setting in.

On the way back to my place, Eddie said, "See, I told you it'd be easy to get laid."

"I know, but I hope it never gets back to Becky."

"Don't worry, Mr. Carpenter. Nobody knows," Eddie said as he laughed. "You've got nothing to worry about, Gary." And I was convinced that he was right.

I had covered my tracks with Debby, and nobody but me, Debby, and my conscience knew what had transpired in that bedroom that day. I had used the alias as a cover, so there was no way the situation could backfire on me. Aside from that, I truly believed that was going to be the only time I'd ever see Debby.

The next night, Becky, my mother-in-law, Mary, and her boyfriend, Mike, showed up at about six, and Becky informed me that she was going to make dinner for the four of us. As she and her mother fixed dinner, I talked to Mike, and he told me about the little country band he was in and how they played all the little bars in town. I mentioned to him that I could play drums, and he suggested that Becky and I make a trip to the bar the next week to hear them play,

I said, "Okay, but don't be surprised if I try out your drums while we're there."

He laughed and said, "If you're any good, don't you be surprised if we offer you a job."

That's how I got started playing music with his band when their regular drummer couldn't make it to a gig. And I kept playing with them until the night of the accident. We played every little hole-in-the-wall tavern in and around Kansas City.

Once I became familiar with the band scene, I met other band members who would ask me to perform gigs with them. Suddenly I was busy every weekend, playing music and making spare money.

However, I more or less got away from Becky's mother's boyfriend, Mike. I didn't like the way he tried to control Becky. It was the same way he controlled every move her mother made. He told Mary where she could go and when she could go there. He and I had several fights about it. I felt that he was a drunk and a loudmouth who talked a lot of trash. He liked to talk about how "bad" he was, and he tried to make everyone think he was as bad as he himself thought he was. When he started trying to lay his controlling hand on Becky by telling her how she should be conducting herself within our marriage, I felt he was out of line. I let him know that if he kept it up, I would punch his lights out. I told him that I was in no way scared of him or any of his friends and that he should keep his mouth shut. After that conversation, we became the best of enemies.

The last gig I played with Mike's band was the night of the accident. It was at a place called the Matador Club over on Twenty-Eighth Street in Kansas City. I remember that night so well. It was not only the night of my near-fatal accident, but earlier in the week I had celebrated my twenty-first birthday. To make the night even more memorable, earlier in the evening one of the band members had gotten into a fight. Another band member and I had to take him to the hospital to get his arm fixed, because he had run it through a glass door. I didn't know it at the time, but in just a few short hours I was going to be lying on a stretcher in that same ER, dying.

After getting the arm looked at, we returned to the bar and played a couple of sets. I was drinking, but I wasn't drunk. However, I guess I did have a high. During a break I called Debby's house and asked if she could get away for the night. Becky hadn't come to the show. She was out of town with her mother, showing my daughter, Dawn, off to some of her relatives. That made it a good time to "get a little," if you know what I mean. By that time, Debby and I had become a regular feature. We had been seeing each other for about six month's. She now knew my real name, and she knew that I was married, but she didn't seem to care. Every time Becky would go out of town, I'd head over to Debby's. Cheating got easier after the first time; the guilt seemed to have worn off.

Debby said that her parents, her mother and her stepfather, had already gone to bed, and she inquired as to when I could be there to pick her up.

I told her I would ask Don, our sixty-something-year-old steel guitar player, if I could use his car to pick her up. I was pretty sure he'd let me, so I told her that I'd pick her up in an hour or so. I went and told Don that I had a hot date to pick up and I asked if I could borrow his car. All the band members got hot dates once in awhile. It was just something that happened when you played music there was sort of an unwritten code among the band members that you cover for each other if the band member was married and messing around.

"It's not my car. I had to borrow it from a friend," he said.

"Oh, come on, Don, let me use it. I told this girl I would be there to pick her up."

"I'm sorry, Tripp, but I'm responsible for that car, and I can't let it out of my sight."

"Okay, then, why don't you ride over there with me to pick her up?"

"Well, okay, let me get Bill. We'll ride in the backseat, and you two can have the front."

Bill was another band member. The three of us had a couple more drinks before we finally piled into the car and headed for Debby's house. Needless to say, by that time we were feeling no pain. The car was an old Studebaker. I don't remember the year, but it had the small windshield. Unfortunately, it was cold that night and the defroster wasn't working very well. I cleared the inside of the windshield with an old, dirty rag that I'd found lying on the floorboard. We picked Debby up and headed back to the Matador Club. As soon as I got back onto I-70, I pushed the gas pedal to the floor and accelerated down the ramp headed west. I understand from what the police told me later that I'd accelerated to a speed in excess of 120 miles per hour in just a quarter of a mile. That was before I blew a tire. I remember reaching for a rag to wipe off the inside of the window, and I remember hearing Debby scream just before everything went dark. When I came to, there was a State Patrol officer bent over me, asking me what my name was and who had been driving the car.

I remember asking, "Where am I?"

The officer replied, "You were in a car accident. What's your name?"

As I lay there trying to clear my head, I felt a warm feeling and a tingling sensation throughout my body. I couldn't move. I felt what must have been blood running down my face. At the same time, it was like I was in a dream world. The officer held a clipboard in his hand and was writing something down.

He repeated, "Who was driving the car?"

Everything was so fuzzy, and then I remembered Debby's scream.

I remember trying to ask the officer, "Where is Debby?"

He didn't have time to give me an answer because the paramedics had started working on me. I passed out as they tried to put me on a stretcher and get me into the ambulance. The next time I awoke, I heard the sound of the siren as I was being driven to the hospital. I remember looking out the back window of the ambulance and seeing a road sign for Twenty-Seventh Street, and even in the condition I was in, I knew where we were. I had traveled that road all my life. I looked over at the paramedic and apparently tried to say something. He responded by saying, "Everything will be okay, Mr. Tripp." I remember thinking, "How does this guy know who I am?" I then passed out again.

At the scene of the accident, during the ride to the hospital, and at the hospital, I kept telling myself this was just a bad dream. It couldn't be real. It was just a bad nightmare. I have no idea how long it took to get me to the hospital or how long I had been there before I regained consciousness. When I did wake up, I was lying on a gurney, trying to vomit up whatever was left in my stomach and the blood I was losing from my injuries. Hospital personnel had positioned me flat on my back on the gurney. This and the oxygen mask covering my face were keeping me from being able to vomit. I opened my eyes and saw my father. I tried to tell him to turn me on my side so I could vomit. He couldn't hear me. He raised the mask, and I think he then understood what I was trying to tell him.

He helped turn me onto my side. As he did, I heard one of the nurses in the room question my father, "What are you doing?"

Before my dad could answer her, she yelled, "Leave that guy alone; he's just going to die!"

I remember my dad yelling back at her as I again passed out, "You're out of your mind, lady."

The damage I did to my body that night was extensive. I was later told that the doctors hadn't thought I would survive. I had broken every bone in my face; I had at least seven broken ribs; and I'd cracked vertebras. My cheekbones were crushed, and my eyes were hanging out of my eye sockets. I had lost all my teeth, and my heart had stopped beating several times, but the doctors had been able to restart it. That nurse might have been right to tell my father that I was going to die. But he wasn't buying it. I don't know how long I was out, but the next time I opened my eyes, Becky was standing at my bedside. Her eyes were full of tears. She looked so hurt and so loving at the same time.

I could see rage in her eyes, and she was pleading with me for answers, "Why Rick? Why? Who was the girl you were with?"

I remember looking at her and trying to tell her that I didn't know who she was talking about. What I didn't know at the time was that Debby had been moved to another hospital just before Becky had arrived to see me. And someone had told Becky that a girl had been in the wreck with me. Never did find out who told her but someone sure did. Because Becky knew that a girl had been with me in the accident. The secret I had kept all those months was now out in the open. I wasn't sure how much Becky knew, but I had an idea she would soon figure out what I'd been up to, and the consequences couldn't be good.

It was about that time that I started to think that this nightmare might actually be real. A lot of thoughts ran through my mind. I wondered if I was going to die; I wondered how bad Debby had been hurt; What I didn't know at the time is that both Don and Bill had been lucky they had been in the back seat of that car when I wrecked it, neither one of them had been hurt in the accident. My thoughts returned to my baby girl I wondered what would happen to my daughter, Dawn Kay, if I died; I wondered who would raise my little girl; and I wondered what I was going to do. My thoughts turned to the look of pain in Becky's eyes and the realization that I'd caused that pain with my actions. I was thinking all those things as I drifted off, and I remember saying a little prayer, "God, please, I don't know if this is real, but please, if it is, don't let me die. I need to be here for my little girl. And by the way, if it is real and you let me make it through, I swear that I'll never mess around on Becky ever again."

I don't know how many days it took before I again regained consciousness, but I heard my mother's voice saying, "Rick, are you awake?"

I tried to open my eyes, but everything was black.

"Mom, I can hear you, but I can't see you," I said.

"I know, Son," was her reply.

"Why can't I see you, Mom? Am I blind? I can't see you."

"You're okay, Son. They had to put some bandages on your eyes. You'll be okay."

About that time, I heard Becky's voice. It was a strange feeling to hear them but not be able to see them. Suddenly my mind started playing tricks on me. It scared me that I couldn't see them through my eyes, but I could see them in my mind. My mother continued to talk. She told me that my eyelids had been sewn shut and that I'd had an operation to remove some of my ribs in order to rebuild my face. She added that I would be able to see again in a few days when the bandages came off.

Becky spoke up, "How you feeling, honey?"

I said, "Not very good. My side is hurting."

"Well, that's to be expected. They'll give you something for the pain."

I then heard someone else say, "Okay, Mr. Tripp, here's something for your pain," and I felt a shot.

My mother chimed in, "Son, we'll be back after a while. Get some sleep."

I was kept pretty well sedated during the several weeks I spent in the hospital. The bandages eventually came off, the stitches were removed from my eyelids, and I could see again. At the time of the accident, my mother was divorced and living alone in her two bedroom house on Ninth and Booth in Kansas City. She let Becky and Dawn move in with her while I was in the hospital. When I got discharged from the hospital, I moved in with her too. I felt bad that my family had to live with my mother, and I didn't like imposing on Mom, but there was nothing else I could do. Becky, Dawn, and I lived there for eight or nine months as I tried to recuperate from the accident.

I was nowhere near being ready to return to work when I was discharged from the hospital. I had a busted jaw and numerous other broken bones in my face. A contraption was hooked to my head to hold all my facial bones together. It included little white buttons above my eyes and wires coming out of my head. I couldn't even eat solid food, and I spent a long time drinking my meals through a straw. It was several months before I could even consider looking for a job.

During this time, my mother had an extremely hard time paying all the bills. She suggested that if Becky wanted to get a job, she could work with her down at the café. It was a railroad café in Kansas City, and it was run by the Southern Pacific Railroad. With Becky working, we could help with some of the bills. Knowing it would also give her some spending money, Becky was receptive to the idea. I personally didn't like the idea, because I knew the café was a place where my wife would meet a lot of guys. Not only that, but I knew the guys going in there made good money and the like. Let's face it; I was scared that Becky would meet someone at the café and that she'd start cheating on me like I'd done to her. We were only barely getting along, and she hadn't completely forgiven me for the fling I'd had with Debby. I didn't need any other factors out there threatening to make my situation worse. But I lost the objection, and Becky started working as a waitress at that café.

A few months went by before I noticed a pin on her bra as she was changing her clothes. I asked her about it, and she said one of the old timers at the café had given it to her.

I asked, "Why in the hell are you wearing it on your bra?"

She avoided my stare and refused to look me in the eyes as she said, "He's just a friend."

Now, I can't prove it, even today, but one of the jobs for the waitresses at that café was to go in and change the linens at the little hotel that was connected to the restaurant. Train personnel stayed at the hotel during their turnarounds if they had put in too many hours and needed to get some rest before they went back to work. I asked her who the train pin she was wearing belonged to, each year the different railroads will give their employees' like engineers' and conductors a gold pin with the number of years they have been in service of that particular railroad company as a keepsake, and that's the kind of pin she had on her bra, but she would never give me an answer about who the pin belonged to. I knew right then that I had a problem, and I had a good idea that someone else was getting the sex I wasn't getting. I decided that Becky was using my fling with Debby as an excuse for not wanting to have sex with me during that time.

Now, the night I was in the accident I made a vow to God that I would never mess around on Becky again. And at the time, I had meant it. But now that I thought Becky was messing around on me, I couldn't see the sense in sitting at home looking at the walls. Aside from that, I had been wanting to call Debby and tell her how sorry I was that I had hurt her in the accident. I had tried to call her a couple of different times, but her stepfather or mother would always answer the phone and say she didn't want to talk to me. One day, when Becky and Mom were at work, I convinced Eddie to drive me over to Debby's house so I could speak to her in person.

Debby's stepfather came to the door and said, "Get off my property. She doesn't want to see you."

I pleaded with the man, "You don't understand. I just want to tell her how sorry I am that she got hurt."

He was having none of it. "I don't care what you want. If you don't leave, I'll call the police."

With that threat, I returned to Eddie's car, and we left.

But a day or two later, Debby called me at my mother's house I talked to her and told her I was doing alright and that I was sorry I had hurt her. One thing led to another, and eventually we decided to meet away from her parents' house. We were soon running around together again. By that time, I had started playing in a band on the weekends. I was making a little money, sneaking out while my mother and Becky were at work, and I was seeing Debby more and more. That went on for a few months before Debby dropped a bomb on me, one that I had not expected.

We were sitting in the car I had just bought, eating hamburgers at one of our meeting spots, when she looked over at me and said, "Rick, I've got something to tell you."

"Oh really, what?"

"I'm pregnant."

"You're what?"

"I'm pregnant."

"You're kidding, right?"

"No, Rick."

"How long have you known?"

"I stopped my menstrual period last month."

"Have you seen a doctor?"

"No."

"Well, maybe it's something else, Debby."

"I don't think so, Rick."

"Does your mom or dad know?"

"Not yet."

"Well, if you are pregnant, then who's the father?"

About the time I said that, she started crying. She jumped out of the car and started walking down the street; she was almost running. I might add that she called me a few choice names and threw in a few other well-chosen words. I finally pulled the car in front of her, jumped out, grabbed her, put my arms around her, and said, "Hey, I was only kidding."

She said, "This isn't anything to be kidding about. You know I've been seeing you for the past couple of months and only you. How could you ask me that question?"

"Like I said, Debby, I was only kidding."

"Well, what am I going to do, Rick?"

"I don't know, Debby, but I'll figure something out," I said.

I gave her a hug and a kiss, talked her into getting back in the car, dropped her off about a block from her parents' house, and told her I would call her later.

Needless to say, I had a lot on my mind after I dropped her off. I wasn't only thinking about her and me, but also about the baby she might be carrying. Maybe she wasn't really pregnant. That was what I was hoping. But if she was, then I was in trouble in more ways than one. Maybe I could rent her an apartment on the side. She and the baby could live there, and Becky would never have to know that I had fathered Debby's baby. If I could make that happen, I could get Debby out of her parents' house without my name ever being brought up. I couldn't let her go through this alone, and I didn't condone abortion. The idea of giving someone money to kill something that was part of me was out of the question, but at the same time, I knew all hell would break loose if Becky ever found out about the baby.

For the next few months I explored the option of moving Debby out of her parents' house and into an apartment where I would help her pay the rent. That's what I had told Debby I wanted to do. I wanted to handle it, at least until I got a divorce from Becky. But I had no intention of ever divorcing Becky.

In the meantime, Debby got a job as a maid at a motel. With the money she earned and the extra money I was giving her, she got an apartment. That went on for a few months, and I thought everything was going to be alright. I was going to keep everything together, and Becky would never find out about the baby Debby was carrying.

In the months that followed, I got well and started back to work full time. I got my family a little apartment, and everything seemed to be going okay. I was helping pay the rent for Debby's place, and at the same time I was taking care of my wife and my baby girl. But things were about to get complicated.

One day I was out with Debby when I decided to stop by my mother's place to see how she was doing. Because Debby was in the car, I parked my car down the street and walked up to my mother's house. My little sister was in the yard. I approached and said, "What's new, Sis?"

She looked up at me with a look of surprise on her face and said, "What are you doing here? You're supposed to be over at your place."

"What do you mean, Pam?"

"Mom, Becky, and Hank are over at your apartment, waiting for you and your girlfriend to show up."

Hank was my stepfather, but he was divorced from my mother at the time.

I said, "Why would they be over there, Pam?"

"Because your girlfriend's mother called Becky today and told her that her daughter was going to have your baby. They're waiting for you two to show up, because your landlord said that while Becky was out of town the other day, you had a woman over there. The landlord said you told him that the woman was your cousin and she stayed all night."

"Okay, Sis, I've got to go. Don't tell anyone that I stopped by, okay?"

"Okay, Rick."

I hurried back to my car and told Debby what had happened. I dropped her off at one of her girlfriends' houses and headed for my apartment. I got there and started up the steps to my apartment. I lived on the second floor, and as soon as my foot hit the stairs, I looked up and saw Becky. She was ready for a fight.

She started screaming, "Where is she?"

I asked, "Where's who?"

"That whore you've been running around with."

"I don't know what you're talking about."

"I know you had her here, Rick. The landlord told me you had someone up here the other night."

"Becky, you've got it all wrong. That was my cousin, Linda. I had her up here trying to help me clean things up the other night."

She didn't believe me. I continued up the steps, and my mother appeared. My mom said, "Okay, where's she at, Rick?"

"Mom, I don't know who you guys are talking about?"

My mother looked at me, and I could tell she didn't believe my story about having my cousin over to help clean my apartment.

I said, "But Mom, you guys can call Linda and find out."

On the way to my apartment, I had called my cousin Linda and asked her to cover for me. She had agreed, but she said that I owed her one.

"Richard, I know when you're lying to me," my mother said. She then looked at Becky and said, "Okay, Becky, get your stuff. Me and Hank will take you and the baby over to your mother's."

"Mom, are you guys nuts? I don't want my baby girl going anywhere. I especially don't want her around that guy her mother lives with," I said as I gestured toward Becky.

"You should've thought of that before you started messing around on your wife, Richard."

My mother only called me Richard when she was mad, and when that little redhead was pissed, you knew to stay out of her way. Because of this, I didn't even try to stop them as they loaded up all of Becky and Dawn's possessions. I wanted to interfere, but it was pointless. They loaded up, took off, and left me in the apartment alone.

Later that night, I was sitting alone when I realized that the unthinkable had happened. My wife and my baby were gone. I was left to ask myself, "What am I going to do now?"

For several days, I attempted to call Becky at her mother's house, but her mother refused to allow me to speak with my wife. About a week later, I drove over to visit Becky and my baby girl. That's when I found out that they'd moved on. They'd taken up residence with Becky's Grandmother Smith in Harrisonville, Missouri, a town that was a good fifty miles from Kansas City. I called there a few times, and Becky's Grandma Smith would tell me that Becky didn't want to speak to me. A few weeks went by before Becky finally got on the phone. I told her that I loved her and missed the baby and would do anything to get them to come home. She refused. She said they were just fine where they were and that she had started back to school to get her GED. All she needed from me was money. She had gotten a part-time job working as a waitress in a restaurant; she planned to apply for food stamps; and she planned to hire a lawyer to represent her as she filed for a legal separation from me.

I said, "But honey, you haven't got to do that. I really love you, and I need you."

"If you want something to love, go get that whore you were running around with," she said curtly before hanging up the phone. She had made it very plain to see what she thought about me and the situation.

In the meantime, Debby and I had one fight after another. I blamed her because I had lost my wife and my daughter. During one night of heavy alcohol consumption, I commented that if Debby's mother hadn't called my wife, my life would have been much better off. That led to a heated argument. Debby got pissed and told me that I should go to my wife. Then I got pissed and informed her that the unborn child she was carrying was the only damn reason I wasn't with my wife in the first place. One thing led to another. By the time the fight was over, a lot of hurtful things had been said, and Debby and I went our separate ways.

It was then that I decided that the only thing I wanted out of life was to get my wife and child back, and that's what I set out to do. A problem arose when I went to a lawyer and received some bad advice. You see, somewhere I'd gotten the idea that if I went down to Harrisonville, got my daughter, and moved her back to Kansas City with me, then Becky would come back to town, and I could show her that I had changed. I went to a lawyer and asked him if my plan would be considered kidnapping. He told me that as long as there hadn't been any court papers filed, Dawn was as much my property as she was Becky's. In other words, Becky and I both had guardianship of Dawn. Armed with this lawyer's advice, I devised a plan to go get Dawn and bring her back to Kansas City. I called Becky, told her that I was going to bring her some cash, and let her know that I wanted to see my baby girl. She agreed to the meeting.

I arrived in Harrisonville, handed Becky some money, and told her that I needed a receipt. I'd planned to drive off with Dawn while Becky was getting the receipt, but I hadn't counted on her grandfather grabbing the car's door handle as I tried to back out of the driveway. If I'd have continued to leave, I would have hurt the old man.

As this commotion unfolded, Becky's grandmother called the city police. The officers arrived on the scene, took my daughter out of my car, and handed her to Becky. Their actions were illegal, but when you're dealing with a crazy country cop who has a gun in your face, you do as you're told. I know now that my plan was crazy, but at the time, I would have done anything to get my wife and baby girl back.

I returned to Kansas City, got my attorney on the phone, and told him what had happened. I also told him that Becky had mentioned filing legal separation papers. He told me that something sounded funny about that, and he questioned why Becky didn't just file for divorce. I assured him that I didn't know.

"Well, do you know who is representing her, Mr. Tripp?"

"No, I don't."

"Well, when and if you find out, give me a call. I'll in turn give him a call and find out what is really going on."

"Okay, I'll call her and ask her who her attorney is."

"Okay, Mr. Tripp, let me know what you find out."

A few days later, I called Becky and asked for the name of her attorney. I relayed the information to my own attorney and waited as he made a call to find out why Becky was filing for legal separation as opposed to filing for divorce. When I found out the reason, I almost had a heart attack. Becky was pregnant and had been when she'd left me in Kansas City. I hadn't known, and I'm quite sure she hadn't known about the pregnancy until after she had moved to Harrisonville and went to see a doctor for a checkup. That is why she had only wanted a separation. The judge wouldn't give her a divorce until after the baby was born. At least that's how the law was back then. When I found out that my wife was pregnant, I again decided that I would do whatever it took to get my family back. I knew I had hurt her more than anyone ought to be hurt. I had a lot of guilt, and I didn't know if she would take me back, but I knew I had to try.

A few days after I found out my wife was pregnant, I was riding down the street with my friend Bill, when we saw a guy walking hand in hand with Debby.

I said, "Just keep driving, Bill."

He responded, "But wasn't that Debby, Tripp?"

I answered, "Yep."

"Well, don't you want to ask her what's going on?"

"No, I have other plans."

He looked a bit puzzled, but he kept driving, and he dropped me off at my place. Seeing Debby walking with that guy, whoever he was, was enough to make me decide that I was going to move to Harrisonville. I figured that if Debby had found a new boyfriend that fast, then she didn't need me, whether she was going to have my baby or not. As far as I was concerned, Debby was on her own.

Shortly thereafter, I was laid off from my job. A situation that normally would have caused me angst, instead proved to be perfect timing. I was able to draw unemployment for a few months. This gave me a check each week and afforded me an opportunity to move to Harrisonville. I moved into an old hotel in Harrisonville into a room that cost about forty dollars a week. This left me about fifty dollars each week for all my other expenses. By the time I gave Becky money, there wasn't much left for me to spend on food. However, I was a determined man, and I made it through the next several months.

I tried every move in the book to win her back. I took her on long walks, talked about getting back together, took her out to dinner. You name it, I tried it, but nothing was working. It was as if she had no real interest in reconciliation, no matter what I did.

Becky spent many weekends at her Aunt Linda's place in Amorite, Missouri, which was about 50 miles away from Harrisonville, while I remained in Harrisonville. I didn't give it much thought at the time, but it later dawned on me that even though she was pregnant with my son, she likely had her own little affair going on. I was so bent on making up for my own adulterous mistakes that the idea of her having an affair was far from my mind. The baby was almost due before I figured out that something might be going on. What I did know was that she didn't want to spend much time with me during the month or two before my son was born. I also knew that we hadn't been sexually active with each other since she had left our place in Kansas City nine months prior. You might say that I was starting to wonder. The idea that another man might be on my wife's mind left me feeling like a sucker.

I returned to my motel room one day and found a message stating that a girl named Debby had called from Kansas City. She had left her number and wanted me to return the call. At first, I had no intention of returning the call. I had decided that things were completely over between Debby and me. At the same time, I was intrigued to learn how she had gotten my phone number. I had learned through some friends that she had given birth to a little girl, whom she'd named Joyce, after her mother. While I had wanted to see the baby, I didn't want to do anything that would jeopardize my chances with my wife and the reconciliation I was still hoping for. I knew that dream would vanish if Becky even thought I was still in contact with Debby. After a long period of contemplation, I decided to make the call and see what was on Debby's mind.

She answered the phone.

I said, "This is Rick. What did you want?"

There was a pause on the other end of the line before Debby said, "I just wanted to tell you about our baby girl."

"So the information I heard was true, then?"

"Well, I don't know. What did you hear, Rick?"

"That you had a little girl and you named her Joyce after your mother."

"Why haven't you tried to come see her?"

"It's simple, Debby. All that stuff we had going on when I left town is history. I'm trying to save my marriage, and I don't need any more problems right now. Besides that, before I left town, Bill and I saw you walking and holding hands with some guy, so I felt like you had your life together."

"So that's why you stopped seeing me?"

"That's one of the reasons, it's kind of hard to forget that your supposed to be carrying my baby but at the same time your holding hands with some guy?" but there were others reasons to …"

"Well, you should have called and asked me who that guy was. You just saw what you wanted to, Rick. That was just a guy who worked with me at the motel."

"Whatever, Debby. So how did you get my number?"

"A friend of yours gave it to me."

"And where are you living now?"

"I'm back at my parents' house. I lost my place, and the money I make isn't enough to take care of the baby and have my own place at the same time," she said.

"So what was the full name you gave the baby on her birth certificate?"

"What you mean, Rick?"

"What's the baby's last name?"

"My stepfather's insurance paid for her birth. I gave Joyce his last name, Gunn, so the insurance at Ford would pay the bill."

"Well, that's just ducky, and you still want me to believe she's my daughter?"

"You know Joyce Ann is yours, Rick."

"Well, I've got to go, Debby."

I hung up the phone. I was pissed. I couldn't believe that her stepfather had the gumption to convince Debby to stick his name on my daughter's birth certificate. Who in the hell did he think he was? I didn't really care why he had done it. The point was that it had happened. No one was going to stick their name on my daughter's birth certificate, period. Debby's stepfather didn't know it yet, but he'd just created a problem for himself, and he might soon be facing one hell of a fight. I had allowed him to shut the door in my face the day I had tried to apologize to Debby for the wreck. But this stunt was too much for my ego to take.

I let that phone call get to me. After several days, I decided to call my old friend Bill, who still lived in Kansas City. I arranged to have Bill pick me up in Harrisonville at the time I didn't own an automobile one night. My plan had been to go up to Kansas City, catch Debby's stepfather going to the store one night, and have it out with him for what he had done. I was basically making the trip to whip his ass. Just in case he was carrying a weapon, I'd stuck my .38 under the passenger seat in Bill's car. I didn't really expect that I would have to use it, but it felt good to be prepared. I had grown up in some of Kansas City's worst neighborhoods. Because of this, I had learned to always carry an equalizer like my 38 special pistol.

As I was getting into the car, Bill asked, "What's the heat for, Tripp?"

"It's just a precaution in case we run into some problems."

"Where we are going?"

"Debby's house."

"Are you out of your mind? You called me down here to go see that tramp?"

"No. I don't really want to see her. I want to pay her stepfather Mr. Gunn a visit."

I then filled Bill in on my plans.

He listened. When I was done, he said, "Tripp, you're playing with fire. Why don't you just forget her and her family?"

"It's just something I have to do, Bill. Are you in, or do I have to call someone else?"

"I don't like it, Tripp, but I'm already here, so let's go do it. But for the record, I think you're crazy."

We headed for Kansas City. The sky was just starting to darken when we pulled up to Forty-third and Ditzler streets. We parked about a block from Debby's house in a spot that allowed us to see her driveway. Her stepfather's car was there, so I decided that he hadn't yet left for the store. Debby's stepfather had a funny way of doing things. One of his quirks was that he bought his groceries by the day rather than by the week. Because of this, I knew he would be going to the store that night. My plan was to follow him, catch him coming out of the store, and confront him about putting his name on my baby's birth certificate.

One of the reasons I'd chosen to call Bill was because he had just bought a new car. It was a little white Mustang, and neither Debby nor her stepfather would recognize it. Bill and I were able to sit and observe what was going on without anyone being the wiser.

After a few minutes had been spent watching the house, Bill said, "Tripp, I think this is a waste of time. Nothing is going on at that house."

About that time, a car carrying a couple of guys drove past us, pulled into Debby's driveway, and honked the horn. Out came what looked like Debby and another girl. They got into the car, it backed out of the driveway, and they took off.

Bill looked over at me, smiled, and said, "Tripp, are you ready to leave? It looks to me like she's going out on a date."

"Let's follow them and see where they go," I said. "The next time I talk to that tramp, I don't want her to be able to say that I only see the things I want to see."

"Okay, but I think you ought to just forget about her." He started the car and we followed the group.

I told him, "Let's stay back a little. I don't want them to know they're being followed."

We ended up at a gas station over on Highway 50. The group parked and went inside. We pulled up, parked across the street, and watched them through the glass that decorated the front of the station. At one point, I saw Debby kiss one of the guys. At that moment, I was ready to leave. She had just given birth to my baby a few weeks ago. I turned my head to look away for a second. As I was thinking to myself about how big a fool I had been, Bill interrupted my thoughts.

"Tripp, I think they saw us. Here come those two guys. You want me to take off?"

"No, I want to hear what they have to say."

I reached under the seat, grabbed my .38, slid it onto my lap, covered it with a piece of newspaper, and sat there with my finger on the trigger. They walked up to the car's passenger-side door.

I rolled the window down and asked, "Can we help you?"

"Are you Richard Tripp?"

"Yes, why?"

"Well, you see that girl in the window across the street?"

"Yep, I see her, so what?"

"Well, she said that you've been bothering her."

"Oh really."

"Yes, and I just want to let you know that my friends and I will whip your ass if you don't leave her alone."

"Oh really," I repeated.

Bill looked over at me and shook his head. He knew I had the .38 in my hand, and he knew how pissed I was. The guy doing the talking kept right on talking. "I run with a bunch of bad dudes. If you know what's good for you, you'll leave her alone."

It took every bit of mind control I had to keep me from shooting him right there. Until this day, that guy has no idea just how close he came to meeting his maker that night. I convinced myself that it wasn't worth it.

Instead, I told the guy, "Okay, we'll leave. And we won't bother her anymore." I looked over at Bill and said, "Let's go."

As we pulled away from the curb, I could see big grins on the guys' faces as they headed back into the gas station. It was as if they thought they had done something big by running Richard Tripp off. I could just imagine what they were telling those girls as we drove off. Debby was looking out the window with a funny look on her face. I think she knew me well enough to know this wasn't over.

Bill said, "Tripp, I thought for sure you were going to shoot that son of a bitch."

I looked at him and said, "Wasn't the right time or place. Too many people around."

"I know, but I've never heard anyone ever talk to you like that without you going off on them."

"Bill, this isn't over; it's just getting started. Pull over at that pay phone."

Those guys and the stunt they'd pulled had changed the focus of my mission for the night. I was no longer interested in confronting Debby's stepfather. My new goal was to find those guys, kick their asses, and show them that they didn't even know what bad was. I called another old friend, Dusty, and told him that I needed him to grab a few of his friends and meet me in the parking lot of the new baseball stadium over on I-70 and Blue Ridge.

"Why, Tripp?" Dusty asked.

I told him what had happened. I told him that I was going to whip a couple of guys who had just told me how bad they were, and I needed backup just in case some of their friends showed.

"Don't worry, Tripp. We're on our way. Sounds like there's going be a rumble tonight."

"You don't know the half of it," I said.

As I started to hang up the phone, I heard Dusty ask, "Do we need any heat?"

"I don't think so … but on the other hand, it probably wouldn't hurt … just in case."

"Okay, Tripp. We're on our way."

I hung the phone up, looked at Bill, and said, "Let's get to the stadium."

"Tripp, she isn't worth it. Listen to me, Bro."

"Bill, this isn't about her anymore. Those guys think they scared me, and they think I'm some kind of punk. This is about my reputation, Bill. It's not about Debby."

Reluctantly, Bill started driving toward the stadium. I guess he figured there was no way to talk me out of my new plan. My mind was made up. When we arrived at the stadium, no one was there. We waited about ten minutes before Dusty and two carloads of his friends pulled in. I got out of the car just about the same time Dusty did, gave him a bear hug, and then started shaking hands with the friends he had talked into joining us.

"How and where is this little rumble going down?" Dusty asked.

"Well, I've been thinking about that, Dusty. As a matter of fact, that's what Bill and I were talking about when you pulled in. Here's my plan. Bill and I will go sit in front of Debby's house and wait for the punks to bring her home. I'll have you guys stake out the corner of Forty-First Street. You can park one car per driveway on each side of the street. When they pull up at her house, we'll make sure that they see us, and we'll take off. With some luck, I think they'll be dumb enough to follow us around that horseshoe street that leads right back to Forty-First Street. I'll have Bill do a cop block the street turn. After the punks go by, you guys can pull out and block their retreat. They won't be able to go anywhere, and we'll have them right where I want them."

"What about the neighbors down there calling the cops, Tripp?" Dusty asked.

"I have friends that live on each side of the street. I'll let them know what's going on. Besides, if we do this right, it will be over in just a minute or two. We can get the hell out of there before the neighbors even know what's going on. I'm sure I can whip those punks' asses in no time flat. But just in case, Dusty, put my .38 in your car so I don't use it if I get mad."

"Okay, Tripp. Let's go rumble."

With that, we headed over to talk to my friends who lived on Forty-First Street. The trap was set. Bill and I went on up to Forty-Third Street, parked in front of Debby's stepfather's house, and waited. I might add that we didn't have to wait very long. By that time, it was about ten o'clock, and it was dark to boot. We saw headlights turn the corner, and we knew Debby was on her way home.

I said to Bill, "Wait until they get right on top of us before you take off."

I grabbed the mic on Bill's CB radio and called Dusty, "Here they come; get ready, Dusty."

"We're ready down here, Tripp. Bring them on."

As soon as the punks saw us parked outside Debby's stepfather's house, they sped up. When they got right on our bumper, Bill took off. Just as I had planned, they were in hot pursuit. Naturally, we were speeding as we took a right-hand turn and continued down the street. As they took the same sharp turn, we heard a loud "pop."

Bill said, "Tripp, are they shooting at us?"

I looked back. Even in the dark I could see a bullet hole in their windshield. It didn't make sense that they would shoot out their own windshield, but I was fairly certain I knew what I was seeing. Naturally, we sped up when we heard the pop. I couldn't help but ask myself, "Why in the hell did I put my gun in Dusty's car?"

Here my enemies had pulled one, and I didn't have mine for retaliation.

"Looks like it, Bill, but we only have a block to go."

We could see the end of the block coming up fast, and Bill suddenly did the cop block the street turn. The driver of the other car slammed on his brakes in an effort to try to stop without running into us. He was able to do so. I jumped out of our car and charged at the punks on foot. As I headed toward the car, the driver threw it in reverse and tried to retreat. To the punks' amazement, I'm sure, two cars, one on each side of the street, pulled out of the driveways behind them. Their retreat had been blocked.

This all happened very fast, and the punks couldn't have know what was going on. I grabbed the handle on the driver's door and pulled the door open. I then looked down and saw that the driver of the punk car had a pistol pointed at my stomach. I said, "You better use it or lose it, bitch." By then, the punk had had enough time to look around and recognize that my friends were approaching with guns drawn. The punk got a funny look on his face just before he decided to drop his gun.

"Why in the hell did you shoot your own windshield out, punk? Did you want to shoot me that bad?" I asked.

"No, it just went off as I was pulling it out of my pants."

"Oh really?"

I grabbed a hold of him, pulled him out of the seat, and hit him.

We got into a scuffle. I hit him a couple of more times and said something along the lines of, "Okay, bitch, whose bad now?" as he was picking himself up off the ground.

The punk in the passenger seat hadn't moved an inch when I'd grabbed his friend. He'd neither moved nor said a word. It was as if we had scared the shit out of him.

Debby, who was still in the car, decided that it was time to intervene. She tried to get out of the car and got really mouthy. She was yelling, "Rick, you can't do this!"

I said, "Bitch, you better not have anything to say about it. You're lucky I don't punch you in the mouth. Shut up, whore, and get your ass back in that car."

At about that time, the car's driver was picking himself up off the street. I grabbed him, pushed him up against the car, and said, "Punk, let me tell you this just one time. That whore had my baby a couple of weeks ago, and I'm going to see her and my kid anytime I want to. Do you understand?"

He said he understood, so I continued.

"Good. Now, you take that bitch back up there to her stepfather's place, and if I ever see you around this area again, next time it won't go so easy for you."

I was just about to let him go when I came up with one more question.

"By the way, punk, how in the hell did you meet Debby in the first place?"

"Her stepfather introduced us," he said. "I work with him at Ford."

"Well, then, you can deliver a message from me to him."

"What?"

"Tell him what I told you. I'm sure he'll get the message. And the next time you think about telling someone how *bad* you are, remember tonight. Now, go drop her off," I said as I gestured toward Debby.

I picked up his gun off the street, dumped the bullets, and tossed it back into his car.

"Now, get in that car, and get the hell out of here."

With that, they took off.

This whole scene had taken place in less than five minutes. As soon as the punks had started up the hill for Debby's stepfather's house, my clan left the area and spent the night partying at Dusty's place. We'd gotten the hell out of Debby's neighborhood just in case someone had called the police. That night, Dusty, Bill, and the rest of the guys were all bragging about how we had scared those punks. We reminisced about how I had kicked the punk's ass, taken his gun, dumped the bullets, and given the empty gun back to him. We partied until about three in the morning before Bill took me back to Harrisonville.

The next morning, I woke with a hangover. I guess it was about ten o'clock. I immediately called Grandmother Smith's house and asked to speak to Becky.

To my surprise, her grandmother said, "Rick, she isn't here. She went into labor last night. She's had the baby, and she's at the hospital."

I asked, "Why didn't someone call me?"

"I don't know, Rick. You'll have to ask her."

As I hung up the phone, I thought to myself, "Of all the times for her to have my son, it had to be while I was in Kansas City getting shot at."

Dick, You Had Better Get This Cripple out of This Car

I was so excited about having a son that I rushed around getting dressed and almost ran over to the hospital. It was about six blocks from the room I'd rented. I stopped and bought some flowers before proceeding on. The doctor had told Becky that she was going to have a boy when they had done a sonogram on her a few months earlier. But there's a big difference between someone telling you what's going to happen and actually seeing something for yourself. It seemed as if I had waited for this day all my adult life. I actually had a baby boy. I walked into the hospital, approached the registration desk, and asked the nurse which room Becky Tripp was in.

She gave me the room number and said, "I'll show you the way. By the way, congratulations. Do you know that you have the biggest baby to be born here in our new hospital so far?"

"No, I didn't know that. How big is he?"

"He's ten pounds, ten ounces, and he's over twenty-two inches long."

She led me to the door of Becky's room. Becky was asleep when I first walked in, but I guess she'd heard me approaching.

She rose up and said, "Well, I have a son."

I wanted to grab her and give her a hug and a kiss, but first I handed her the flowers. When I got close enough to give her a kiss, she turned her head like she didn't want one.

With that, I sat down in the chair next to her bed and asked, "Honey, why didn't you call me when you had to come here last night?"

"Well, my Aunt Linda brought me, and I didn't see any sense in calling you. There wasn't anything you could've done."

"Well, if you'd have called me, I would have been here for you, Becky."

She didn't respond. After an uncomfortable lull in our conversation, I finally asked, "So where have they got our son?"

"They'll be bringing my son to me in a few minutes so I can feed him."

"I can't wait, Becky," I said excitedly.

"You'll see him in a little bit," she replied.

From the way she was acting, I got a feeling that she'd have been just as happy if I wouldn't have been there. To say the least, it wasn't a good feeling.

The nurse walked in and said, "Mrs. Tripp, are you ready to feed your son?"

"Yes, nurse," Becky replied.

The nurse walked out of the room for just a second before she returned carrying my son. He was all wrapped up in a baby blanket, and he was a big bundle. The nurse handed the baby to Becky before leaving the room. I bent over to look at him as Becky took the blanket off his head. He let out a big cry, and Becky started to feed him. I just sat there and tried to have a conversation with her.

I said, "Well, honey, what are we going name him?"

"I've already named him," she responded flatly.

"You have? What did you name him?"

"Keith Lesley Tripp."

"Where did you come up with that name?"

"I named him after your brother and my brother."

"Well, I guess that's okay, but I had a name I wanted to run by you. I was hoping you might use it."

"I don't want to hear it, Rick. This is my son, I'll name him, and it's already been done."

"Well, if you feel that strongly about it, then I guess his nickname will be 'KLT.'"

As she finished feeding Keith, I asked, "Can I hold him for a minute, Becky?"

"I don't guess it would hurt," she said, as she handed me the baby.

That was the first time I got a really good look at how big he was, and he was smiling when she handed him over. I can't really put into words how I felt as I held him. A man can only once hold his firstborn son for the first time. I believe that all fathers have probably experienced the same feelings I felt that day. When the nurse came in to retrieve the baby, I didn't want to let her take him from me.

As soon as the nurse took him away, I tried again to have a conversation with Becky. I tried to convince her that now that we had a son, we ought to get a place together. We could live there in Harrisonville or maybe move back to Kansas City, where I knew I could find work.

She said, "Rick, I don't want to talk about any plans right now. I'm tired."

I said, "Okay, I'll leave for now, but I'll be back later. Do you want me to bring you anything?"

"No, I have everything I need."

I bent over to give her a kiss, and just as she had done before, she turned her lips away. I kissed her on the cheek and said, "I'll see you later, honey."

"I love you," was the last thing I said to her before I walked out of the room.

As I walked back to my room that day, a lot of thoughts ran through my mind. I was happy that I had a son. I couldn't help but think about how we could go fishing and hunting together when he got older. These were things my father never did much with me because he was always working. But I had such wonderful plans for my son. I was daydreaming about the things most fathers think about. I was going teach him everything from baseball to driving, and I would watch him grow up and become a respected professional. Maybe he'd become a doctor or a lawyer. Maybe he'd fulfill my own little dream and become a police officer. It was a dream I hadn't been able to pursue because of my disabilities I had always had from the time I had polio when I was a child. Or, even better than that, maybe he'd be a Secret Service agent like my grandfather had been. Many possibilities ran through my mind as I walked back to my rented room.

But by the time I reached my room, reality had set in. I was depressed because of the way Becky had acted at the hospital and the way she had shut me up when I mentioned getting back together. I knew that in order to fulfill any of the dreams I had for my son, I would first have to put my family back together. Lurking in the back of my mind was a terrible thought. The way Becky was acting made me wonder if reconciliation was out of the question.

For several weeks after Keith was born, I spent as much time with Becky and the kids as she would allow. We would go on long walks in the city park and around Harrisonville. Naturally, the subject I always wanted to discuss included getting a place where the four of us could live together.

Just as she'd said in the hospital, she reiterated, "I don't feel like talking about it. I'm doing fine at my grandmother's."

That went on for a couple of months. So much time had gone by that I finally decided that we *had* to talk about our current living situation. I broached the subject one day when we were out for one of those walks in the park. As my family sat down for a picnic lunch, I said, "Becky, I really need to talk about our future."

I explained to Becky that my unemployment money would be running out in a couple of weeks and that I wouldn't be able to stay in the room I'd been renting. "I'll have to move back to Kansas City to find a job and to get us a place," I said.

"Well, Rick, I don't want to leave here," she said.

"But Becky, what about our plans to get a place?"

"Rick, those are your plans. I'm just not ready for a commitment," she replied.

"Commitment, my ass, Becky. You're my wife and those are my kids."

"That may be," she said, "and maybe someday I will return to the role of wife, but not right now. Right now we are legally separated."

"But Becky, I don't want to leave Dawn and Keith down here. They're my kids. I love them and you, and I want to be close to all of you."

"Well, Rick, you can always come down and see them on the weekends, after you get a job."

"But Becky, honey, that isn't the same thing," I pleaded.

"Well, I'm sorry, Rick, but that's how I feel right now. And by the way, me and the kids are going out of town in a month or two. We're taking a summer vacation. We'll be visiting my Aunt Linda for a couple of weeks. I'll let you know when, but for the next month or so, if you do decide to move back to Kansas City, you can still come down to see the kids here." She made it very clear that I wasn't wanted around her Aunt Linda's house

Leaving Becky and the kids at Becky's grandmother's house that day felt horrible. I felt like my world had ended. I had pretty much lost all hope of getting my family back together. I didn't want to leave Harrisonville, but I didn't have a choice. The unemployment checks were going to stop coming whether I liked it or not. A week later, I moved back to Kansas City by myself. I was without my wife, my babies, and I'm sure, part of my soul.

I spent a couple of weeks looking for employment in Kansas City and ended up working out of some of the day-labor pools. I basically earned enough money to survive. On Saturdays and Sundays I would hitchhike back and forth to see Becky and the kids in Harrisonville. One Sunday I was hitchhiking back to Kansas City when a guy pulled over and picked me up.

He said, "Where you headed?"

"Kansas City," I told him.

"Well, I'm headed for Kansas City, but I have to stop in Independence for a while and feed my parents' horses. I can drop you on Highway 24 if you'd like. Or, if you've got time to wait for me to feed the horses, I can take you on into Kansas City when I'm done. Whichever way you want to do it is fine by me. What's your name?"

"Tripp," I replied.

"Well, my name is Cliff."

"Nice to meet you, Cliff, and I've got the time if you're going to run me on into town after you're done feeding the horses. What kind are they, anyway?"

"They're Tennessee walking horses," he said.

"Sounds like they're nice horses."

"Yep, my mother and father have had them for a few years."

We talked as he drove along, and soon we were pulling into his parents' driveway.

"You might as well stretch your legs while I get my chores done," he said.

"Okay, Cliff. They sure are some good looking animals."

"Hey, Tripp, do you want to ride one while I'm busy?"

"Well, sure."

"Have you ever ridden before?" he asked.

"Sure. I used to ride at Benjamin's Stable out by Slope Park when I was a kid."

"Okay, you know how to saddle him?"

"Sure do."

"Well, the saddles are in the barn. Have fun."

I walked into the barn, got a saddle, put it on one of the horses, and started riding him across the field. I have never figured out what happened that day, but something spooked that horse, and he started running. He ended up running up onto the pavement of the highway in front of Cliff's parents' house, and as soon as he hit the blacktop he reared up and threw me off. I knew as soon as I hit the pavement that something was wrong. My legs felt numb, but when I tried to move them, there was excruciating pain from my waist area. My legs just wouldn't move. It was like I was paralyzed from the waist down.

Cliff had seen what had happened. He rushed over and tried to help me stand up, but the pain was just too much. I couldn't move.

I told him, "Go get the horse and put him up. I'll lay here until you get that done. Then bring your car over. I'll try to crawl in it, and you can drop me off at my mother's place."

Cliff finally pulled the car around. With his help, I grabbed the door and made it into the seat. Getting into that car had hurt badly, but once I was situated in a sitting position it didn't hurt much unless I moved. I should have had Cliff take me straight to the hospital, but I didn't want to go there until I had let my mother know what had happened. She was expecting me back that evening, and I didn't want her to worry. When we got to her house, I sent Cliff to the door to tell her I was in the car.

She came out to the car, and I said, "Mom, I've got a big problem."

"What's wrong, Rick?" she asked.

I told her what had happened, and she replied, "Why in the hell didn't you go to the hospital?"

"Well, Mom, I thought you would want to know what happened."

She shook her head and said, "Rick, you should have gone straight to the hospital. I've got no way of moving you out of that seat, especially if you're hurting like you say you are. Why don't you go over to your father's place and see if he can help get you out of the car. Although, I really think you should head to the hospital, Son."

"I'll have Cliff take me over to Dad's and see what he says. I'll call you later, Mom."

"Okay."

My father only lived about four blocks from my mother's house, so I had Cliff take me over there. When we arrived, my stepmother, Nancy, was watering the grass. I motioned for her to come over to the car door so I could speak to her.

"What in the heck are you out doing, Son?" she asked.

"Mom, I think I'm in big trouble?"

"What's wrong, Rick?"

I told her what had happened. I also told her how I had stopped by my other mother's house and that she had suggested I check to see if Dad could help me out of the car.

Nancy shook her head and yelled to my father, "Dick, you better get out here and get this cripple out of this car."

I let the car door open and moved just a slight bit. The pain was unbearable.

I said, "Forget it, Mom. I'm going have Cliff take me to General Hospital. Have Dad call over there and check on me in an hour or two."

My dad was just coming out the door as Cliff and I pulled off.

I said, "Cliff, I'm sorry about all this. I thought I could make it without going to the hospital, but the pain is too much."

"Don't worry, Tripp. I'll get you there."

When we arrived at the hospital, he went in and got some attendants. They lifted me out of the car, put me on a gurney, and took me inside.

By the time they got me inside, I was really hurting. As soon as the doctor walked into the room, I said, "Doc, please give me something for the pain."

"What's the problem?" he asked. He started examining me and soon noticed that every time I moved, even if it was just a tiny bit, I let out a yell.

I heard him say, "Nurse, give him a shot of Demerol."

I was still in pain after I got the shot.

The doctor said, "Mr. Tripp, we're going take you to X-ray. We're going to take some pictures and see what's wrong with you."

"Okay, Doc."

Cliff said, "I have to go, but I'll call to check on you later, Tripp."

"Thanks for all the help, Cliff," I said.

Cliff left as the hospital staff wheeled me up to X-ray. The shot had started to take effect, but after turning this way and that on the X-ray table, I once again felt like I'd never been given a shot. I was in so much pain. After an hour or two, I was wheeled back down to the ER.

The doctor came in with the X-rays and said, "Mr. Tripp, I hate to have to tell you this, but we're going to have to admit you."

He was looking at the X-rays, and he pointed some areas out to me.

"You see these light areas?" he asked. "Well, that's your pelvis. Where those lighter shades are, those are cracks in your pelvis. Looking at this film, there is also a chance you have some cracked vertebras."

"No, Doc, those cracked vertebras are from a car wreck I was in a while back."

"Actually, Mr. Tripp, I think these are more recent injuries. At any rate, you're going to have to stay off your feet for a few months, and we're going to have to put you on a support that keeps you from moving around while you're healing."

"But Doc, I can't be here that long."

"Mr. Tripp, it's my opinion that you do not have a choice. If you mess around, you could end up paralyzed. Nurse, give him another shot."

With that, the doctor left the room. I was admitted and moved up to Northwest 2. There were no private rooms at General Hospital in those days. The hospital had wards. Each included a line of beds on each side of a big hall. At any given time, there were fifty to sixty patients assigned to each ward. I had been assigned to this ward many times during my life. It was like my home away from home. I had been born in this hospital, and I'd spent so much of life within the hospital's walls that most of the staff knew me on sight. There was no phone for me to use to call my parents, but I was comfortable here. I just laid back and waited for my father or mother to call the hospital. They could talk to the doctor or the head nurse and learn what the diagnosis had been. Eventually, I fell asleep.

My Worst Fears Realized

I was awakened by a nurse taking my blood pressure. "Good morning, Richard. And how are we this morning?"

I looked up and saw Old Lady Hall. Although she was an adult and the head nurse on Northwest 2, I'd known her since I'd been a teenager. She had treated me every time I'd ended up in that hospital. For twenty years or more, she had been the head nurse on that ward. She was a short, little, old, black lady. She must have been in her sixties, but she knew her job, and she knew how to take care of her patients. Although she could get you riled, she had everyone's respect, because the patients knew she really cared about them, their health, and their recovery.

Jokingly, she asked, "So what brings you back this time?"

"Didn't you see the chart?" I responded.

"Are you trying to get smart with me, young man?"

"No, ma'am."

"That's better. Yes, I saw the chart. What were you trying to do, be John Wayne?"

"No, ma'am."

There weren't too many people that I would speak to like that, with respect, but speaking to Old Lady Hall was a lot like speaking to your grandmother.

"Richard," she continued, "a couple of people called to check on your condition last night, and your father said to tell you he would stop by after he got off work tonight."

In my whole life, very few people have addressed me as Richard. Most people called me Rick or Tripp, but Old Lady Hall was an exception. She was one of the few I allowed to address me that way.

"Thank you for the info, ma'am. Could you please get me a pain shot? I'm starting to hurt again."

"I'm not surprised," she replied. "I'll be back in a couple of minutes with a shot."

I was laid out on a bed that had a board under the mattress; a pulley system kept me from moving very much. I didn't even have a pillow. They wanted me to lie flat on my back for the duration of my hospital stay. I didn't have many visitors during those couple of months. Of course, my mother and father came to visit, but that was about it. My wife didn't even make an appearance. About all I could do was lie there and think about my life, my wife, and my kids.

The Sunday I'd been thrown by that horse, I had also gotten into a fight with Becky. She had told me that she and the kids were going down to her Aunt Linda's place for a few weeks, and I wouldn't be allowed to see the kids while she was there, because her aunt didn't want me around. I had once gotten into a scuffle with one of her Aunt Linda's sons. He and Becky had been playing around out in the yard, and I felt that this particular cousin was touching her in a manner that was more becoming of a boyfriend than a cousin. I confronted them about it, and he told his mother. Since that day, her Aunt Linda and I have been enemies.

You might say that Becky and I were not on the best of terms when I left Harrisonville that last Sunday. Before I left, I made the remark, "What, you and your cousin got something going on down there?"

She, in turn, opened her grandmother's front door and said, "You can leave now."

"What, Becky, did I touch a nerve or something?" I prodded.

She didn't answer my question. She simply said, "We'll be back in a couple weeks."

As I lay there in that hospital bed, I started to think that maybe something really was going on. I had wined and dined her the entire time we were both living in Harrisonville. I had become her yes-man. I had done everything I could think to do to prove that I loved her and really wanted to be with my family. Yet all I'd gotten out of her was, "I'm going to see my aunt."

Yes, the more I thought about it, the more I wondered just what was going on at her Aunt Linda's house. Unfortunately, I was about to find out, and my worst fears were about to materialize.

While I was in the hospital, my wife was busy. My father brought me a letter that had been addressed to me at his address. It was from the court, and it advised me that a divorce between me and Becky Tripp had been granted. It also advised me that she had been granted custody of the minor children. In later years, my father admitted that he thought it was a lousy thing for Becky to do while I was cooped up in the hospital. He also told me that I turned as white as a sheet when I read the letter. I must admit that the letter put me in a deep depression. There wasn't anything I could do about the situation at the time; I was confined to that bed in that hospital.

What hurt more than anything else was knowing that my kids might be calling another man "Daddy." That hurt way down in my soul, and then the hurt turned into hatred. I reminisced about all those months I had tried so hard to turn our situation around and all the times I had allowed Becky to walk all over me. It was hard to comprehend that someone I had loved with my whole being, I now hated the same way. I was confined to that bed for a couple of more weeks after I got the letter. I spent most of that time asking, "Why, God? Why me?" and feeling sorry for myself.

Then, out of nowhere, the last person I expected to see in that hospital ward walked in. I saw Debby walking toward my bed. I initially thought I was dreaming, and to tell the truth, I was shocked. I hadn't spoken to Debby once since the night I'd confronted her punk friends and sent them up the hill to her stepfather's house with their tails between their legs.

She walked up to my bed and said, "I heard you were here. How are you feeling?"

"Who told you I was here?"

"Does it matter?" she asked.

"Yes it matters. I haven't even thought about you since the night I caught you with those punks."

"Rick," she said smiling, "are you sure about that? I heard that you were talking to one of your friends just the other day and my name came up."

I thought about that statement for a minute and said, "Okay, where did you run into Eddie?" Eddie had stopped by to see me just one time a few days before, and I think I had mentioned Debby's name in our conversation the day he was here.

"I didn't see him, but he recently went out with one of the girls I work with. She said he mentioned that a friend of his was at General Hospital. The patient's name happened to be Richard Tripp, so I thought I'd stop in and see if it was you."

"Okay, you saw. It's me."

"I also heard that Becky divorced you."

"Boy, you just know all kinds of information."

"I keep my ears open for information about people I care about."

"I'm sure, Debby. And you care so much about me that I caught you with that punk the last time I saw you. You were calling me all kinds of names."

"I know what you think about that, Rick."

"Oh really?"

"Yes, but you don't know what was really going on."

"Really?" I said sarcastically. "What was really going on then?"

"I had to go out with that guy because my stepfather set it up."

I thought about what she'd said and remembered that the punk had told me that he worked at Ford with Debby's stepfather. There was a chance that she was telling the truth.

I gave her the benefit of the doubt and changed the subject.

"So, where are you working?"

"I'm a dancer down on the strip."

Those words conjured up an undesirable vision in my mind. The only girls who danced on the strip were strippers. If she was doing that, then I didn't think much of her new job.

"Oh, well I hope you're making lots of money."

"How come you haven't asked about our daughter, Joyce Ann? You know she's crawling now."

"Oh really? If she's really my daughter, why didn't you bring her down to see me?"

"Rick, I don't even want to go there. I assure you, she's yours. Anyway, I've got to get on downtown. I'll stop by again when I get a chance. We really should talk."

"Whatever, Debby. See you next time."

She left. I assumed that the way I'd spoken to her had hurt her feelings. At the same time, I felt justified. I decided that I was just returning the disrespect she'd shown me during our last encounter. It dawned on me later that I had probably taken my frustrations out on her when I should have been taking them out on someone else. I still had Becky and the kids on my mind.

Debby never did come back to the hospital, not that I blamed her. A few weeks later, I was discharged. A week or two after that, I was back to playing the drums on the weekends and working the labor pools during the day. The first thing I'd done when I got out of the hospital was try to find out what Becky and my kids were up to. I called her Grandmother Smith's house in hopes of speaking with Becky and maybe my daughter, Dawn. Keith wasn't yet old enough to talk.

When Grandma Smith answered the phone, I asked to speak to Becky. She said, "I'm sorry, Rick, but Becky doesn't live here anymore."

"Well, where are she and the kids living?"

"With her aunt."

"Okay, thank you."

I hung up. I didn't even have to ask which aunt. I knew where Becky was staying. I also knew it would be next to impossible for me to visit my kids without trouble from her Aunt Linda and Becky's other relatives down in that little, one-horse town. The only chance I had of finding out anything about my family was through my brother-in-law Ken, and his wife, Nelly. My brother-in-law was Becky's half brother. He and his wife didn't hang out with the side of Becky's family that Becky was currently residing with. However, I still had hope that one of them might hear bits and pieces of information about my ex-wife and children. I was also hoping that they'd be willing to share the information with me.

One night I decided to head down to the strip and see if I could find where Debby was working. In the second bar I entered, there was Debby up on stage dancing, and as I'd suspected, stripping. When she saw me, she about fell off the stage. After she finished her dance, she came over and asked, "What are you doing here?"

"I just thought I'd catch the show," I said.

"Well, my shift is over now. Do you want to go have supper with me?"

I thought about it for a minute and said, "Why not. Let's go down the street to the Pioneer Grill."

We did a lot of talking during dinner. I learned that Debby was still living in her mother and stepfather's house. Her mother watched Joyce Ann while Debby worked. I actually learned a lot about our daughter that day. I even saw a picture of her.

When we finished with dinner, Debby said, "Rick, I've got to get home."

"How do you get back and forth between work and your stepfather's place?" I asked.

"I take a cab home, but he brings me to work," she said. "I've really got to go. Will you come see me tomorrow, Rick?"

"Where?"

"Meet me here at four o'clock. I don't start dancing at the club until six."

"I'll think about it, Debby."

She started out the door, then turned around, ran back to where I was seated, planted a kiss on me, and said, "I'll give Joyce Ann a kiss for you. Bye." She then turned around, rushed out the door, jumped in a cab, and was gone.

That one kiss started me thinking that maybe, just maybe, she still cared about me. Maybe she had told the truth. Maybe she'd really been on a date that had been set up by her stepfather when I'd caught her out that night.

I met her at the Pioneer Grill the next night. From that moment on, we were again dating. It took a lot of work, but I was able to convince Debby to bring

Joyce Ann to see me at a park not far from her parents' house. It was hell having to sneak around to see Debby. She didn't want her stepfather or her mother to know that she was seeing me, and she really didn't want them to know that she had snuck my daughter out to meet me. She said she was afraid they would throw her out of their house if they found out. They apparently had an intense hatred of me since the day I'd almost killed Debby in that car wreck. In a way, I understood. But at the same time, Joyce Ann was my daughter, and I didn't like the idea that someone would try to keep her from me, especially at a time when I was missing my other children.

Becky's relocation had made seeing Dawn and Keith almost impossible. But there was Joyce Ann, right there in Kansas City. I could see her without too much of a fight, and holding her made up for some of the pain I experienced when I couldn't hold my other children. At least I could now hold one of my babies.

The first time I held Joyce Ann, I decided she was mine. I decided that I was going to do everything in my power to have her with me all the time. I knew that wasn't going to happen so long as Debby still lived with her parents. I was also aware that having Debby move in with me didn't necessarily mean that her mother and stepfather would let her have the baby. There was only one surefire way to get my daughter out of that house. Debby and I would have to get married. That would give me legal grounds to fight her parents for custody of my daughter. It would almost guarantee that I would be able to raise Joyce Ann and watch her grow up. I figured that since her stepfather had Debby put his name on my daughter's birth certificate that they might have a legal way of keeping the baby, but if I was married to Debby it would give me an edge if her parents tried something. In today's world we have DNA tests and the like to prove she was mine that I could have used in a court preceding, but back in 1971 we didn't have them, so marrying Debby was the only solution I could think of.

I'll admit that this was a radical plan, and implementing it would require that I make a lot of changes. But at the time, it was the only plan I had. I also knew that I was putting the cart before the horse—Debby had told me that she loved me, but that didn't mean she would marry me.

I couldn't help but think that even if she did agree to marry me, I might still be in trouble. I really didn't know how much of what she told me was the truth and how much was trash. I had caught her running around with a couple of different guys during our relationship. In my eyes, that was a definite reason not to marry her. And, yes, I had talked her into bed just after I met her; and, yes, maybe she was too easy; but maybe that was because she never thought anybody really cared about her. Although people called her a tramp, I thought that maybe I could change her. Maybe providing a good home, love, and affection would keep her from needing anybody else, and maybe we would live a happy life together forever. Boy, was I dreamer. Although I had my doubts, I never would have thought I was about to jump out of the pan and into the fire. I had made up my mind. I was going to ask Debby to marry me.

At about that same time, I decided that I needed to make some other radical changes in my life. I had three obstacles to overcome before I could propose: money, transportation, and new employment.

I had learned the hard way that working in a factory for minimum wage wasn't a very good way to provide for one's family. Sure, factory workers were able to pay the rent, but there was never much money left for anything else. And while playing in a band on the weekends was a lot of fun, it really didn't bring in much money. During our marriage, Becky and I had had many problems and many fights. Looking back, I could see that most were about money.

A second problem Becky and I had faced involved reliable transportation. As a married couple, Becky and I had only owned old junk cars. Not having reliable transportation also led to fighting. I knew that I had to find reliable transportation before I could ask Debby to marry me.

The third problem was twofold. I needed to find viable employment at a job that didn't require me to spend much time on my feet. The injuries I'd sustained in the multiple accidents I'd endured were starting to affect my endurance. My legs were hurting more and more, and I'd begun to notice that I couldn't stand for very long before my feet would start to swell. I needed to find a job that would keep me off my feet.

I racked my mind for several days, trying to figure out how to solve all three problems. I finally came up with a solution. I was going to drive a taxi.

It was a job. I'd be off my feet. I'd have reliable transportation, and all the people I had talked to had told me taxi drivers made a good living.

Taxi Time

I'll never forget the day I walked into Tommy's Cab Company on the corner of Eleventh and Troost Streets in downtown Kansas City. The company was housed in an old, two-story building, and it ran a fleet of about eighty cabs. The building had been used for years as a taxicab stand. I had heard that it also doubled as a mob hangout in the 1920s. When I arrived, the company was owned by a guy named Tommy, a man of Italian descent. One of his brothers, Angelo, was a dispatcher for the company. Another brother, Tony, filled the cars with gasoline, checked the oil, and performed minor maintenance on the fleet. They had the office on the bottom floor of the building. That's where the drivers would pick up their car keys and their trip sheet to mark down their fares. The trip sheet was a record for the city. The cops could go through them, find out when and where you picked up a fare, where they went, and how many people had gone along for the ride. Tommy's office was also located on the building's bottom floor. The upstairs was used as a body shop.

The day I made my first appearance at the cab company, I was as green as could be. I walked in as Tommy was cussing out one of his drivers. He was telling him that if he did something again, he'd take his .38 out and put a bullet in him. I never found out if he would really do something like that, but I heard a lot of different stories.

After overhearing parts of Tommy's conversation, I turned around and started back out the door I had just come in. Tommy saw me and asked, "What you need, kid?" I told him that I had come to fill out an application to be a taxi driver. Just then another driver approached, and Tommy started yelling at him too. I decided it was time to leave. Tommy seemed like a crazy man. He saw me start to back away and said, "Okay, kid, go on in there. Go in my office. I'll be in there in a minute."

I didn't know it at the time, but Tommy's bark was much bigger than his bite. His brother, Tony, wasn't much different, except he used a lot more cuss words. I went into the office and waited. After about ten minutes, Tommy walked in and sat behind his desk. He looked at me and said, "So, you want to be a cab driver?"

"Yes," I replied.

"Do you know the city?" he asked.

"Well, when I was young we moved around a lot, so, yes, I think I know the city pretty good."

"You ever drive a cab for anybody?"

"Nope, but I'm a fast learner," I replied.

He looked at me like he thought I was full of it. "Okay, let me see your hack license."

"My what?" I asked.

Just then, a dispatcher named Jimmy walked into the office. Tommy said, "Jimmy, you see what I have to put up with? This kid wants to drive a cab, and he hasn't even gone down to get his hack license?"

Tommy looked back at me and said, "Kid, what you have to do is go down to the police station, get the police to run a check on you for warrants, take that over to City Hall, give them ten dollars, and they'll give you a hack license."

Seeing the confused look on my face, Tommy asked, "What's wrong?"

"Well, to tell you the truth, I haven't got ten dollars, sir."

He looked at Jimmy, the dispatcher, and shook his head.

"Can you believe the kids today, Jimmy?" He looked back at me and said, "Okay, here's the ten dollars. You go on down, get the papers, come back, and I'll put you to work. You can pay me back when you get your first check."

I took the money and headed to the police station. When I got there, I went through all the formalities one must endure before becoming a Kansas City, Missouri taxi driver. They check your driving record, they check you for warrants, they record your fingerprints, and they take your mug shot for your hack license. Anyone wanting a hack license in those days also had to submit three reference letters from people who'd known them for at least three years, and they had to get a physical from a doctor.

After jumping through all these hoops, the potential taxi driver then had to wait three days for the city to issue the hack license. Three days after I'd jumped through all the required hoops, I returned to the police station and picked up my hack license. I guess you could say I was excited when I picked it up. I knew this was going to be a new opportunity for me. I was not only going to be making good money, I'd also be driving a new car, not a Junker like I had always driven in the past. I took the hack license to the cab company, walked up to the dispatcher's window, informed the dispatcher I was returning with my license, and said that I needed to see Tommy.

He said, "Have a seat, and I'll tell him you're here."

I arrived at shift change, so I sat there for a few minutes, watching the drivers come and go and watching them sign in and sign out their assigned cars. The drivers who had just finished their shifts were turning in their trip sheets and the money they'd made to the cashier.

Back then, there were basically two shifts for taxi drivers. Both were twelve hours long. One shift ran from six in the morning to six at night. The other ran from six at night to six in the morning. A few drivers worked part-time hours, but there weren't many of those. Tommy came out of his office, signaled for me to join him, and walked back inside.

I followed him in. "You got your paperwork?" he asked.

"Yes, sir, here it is," I said.

He looked at it and said, "Okay, everything appears to be in order. Welcome to the cab company. Now, there are a few rules you're going to have to follow. Rule number one: when it's time for your shift to start, be here. If you're not here, your car will be given to another driver. Rule number two: you're not allowed to have people riding with you if they're not a paying customer. That means you will not take your girlfriend out joyriding with you. Are you clear?"

"Yes, sir."

"There are a lot of other rules you'll learn as you go, but breaking this next rule will get you fired in a heartbeat. There is to be absolutely *no* high-flagging," he said.

"Sir, what is high-flagging?"

"That's when you have someone in the cab and the meter isn't on. Every time you have a passenger in that taxi, that meter *has* to be running. And I assure you, the police watch our cabs just for that reason. Do you see the lights on the roof of each of our cabs? The drivers refer to those as snitch lights. When that meter is running, the lights go out. If the police see you with a passenger in your cab while your snitch lights are still on, they will pull you over and give you a two-hundred-dollar ticket. They will also inform us, and you'll be fired. Do I make myself clear?"

"Yes, sir."

"Okay, kid. That's enough of the rules for now. I'm going to let you ride with one of our older drivers. He can teach you the ropes and teach you the other rules."

He picked up his phone, called the dispatcher, and told him to send in Mike. A few minutes later, Mike entered the office.

"You wanted me, boss?" Mike asked.

"Yes, this is Tripp. I want you to train him and show him the ropes."

"Okay, boss. Come with me, Tripp."

Mike was a short, stocky, white guy who later told me that he had been driving a cab for about ten years. He stopped at the dispatcher's window on the way to his taxi, picked up a sign that read "driver trainee," stuck it in the cab's front windshield, and we were off. I learned a lot from him in that one night. He taught me how to use the radio, how to fill out the trip sheet, and a lot of other things I needed to know about driving a taxi. He also taught me which areas to frequent and which areas I should steer clear of.

"Did Tommy give you the talk about the high-flagging?" he asked.

"Yes, he did."

"Well, I'll show you a trick that you'd probably learn on your own anyway, but don't tell anybody I showed it to you."

"Okay, what is it?"

"If ever there's a time when you're giving a friend a free ride and you don't want to be pulled over by the cops, you can turn your key forward like you are trying to just barely turn your car on and the snitch lights will turn off. Now, don't do it very much. It could affect the starter on your car, but it will work in an emergency if you need to avoid getting a ticket."

I finished my shift with Mike, and the next night I was turned loose in my own taxi. It didn't take me long to learn where to pick up fares and how to make a little extra money by high-flagging on the side. What you did was quote people a flat rate for their fare and pocket the money. No one was the wiser because the fare didn't appear on the meter. And in case you ran into the police you could turn on the switch to deactivate the snitch lights.

You Can't Leave Me with These Taxi Drivers

I was sitting at the intersection of Twelfth and Central. At the time, this was known as the Kansas City strip. On one side of the street there was a line of strip bars, and back then this was where the action was. On the other side of the street there was a little park. The Radisson Hotel was also located in this general vicinity. Most taxi drivers knew they could usually pick up a fare with relative ease in this part of town. On this particular day, I had been driving the taxi for about a week. I was sitting there hoping for a good fare when the two-way radio in my cab came to life. A police dispatch statement was being issued.

In those days, the Kansas City Police Department would send out informational dispatches to the cab companies. The dispatchers would then pass the message on to the drivers. If a driver saw the person or people the police were looking for, they could in turn report the sighting to their dispatcher. The dispatcher would then call the police with the information. This particular message said that a robbery had just occurred at Ponaks, one of the bars on the southwest side of the city. The police were looking for the getaway car and the man who was responsible for the robbery. The dispatch said that the man was last seen headed eastbound on Southwest Boulevard, and it was believed that he had a hostage. To tell you the truth, I was a little bored that night.

That message caught my attention and ended the boredom. I found myself wondering, "If I had just robbed Ponaks, how would I escape?" I decided that if I knew someone had seen the direction I had fled, I would double back and go the other way, if it was at all possible. But in that area, it might be just as good to go up into the projects, lose the police, and then double back.

I left the strip and headed over to the intersection of Twentieth Street and Central. I parked on the corner and waited to see if the car the police had described would take the route I thought it might. If it did, I could call the dispatcher and let him know. I sat there on the northwest corner of that intersection with my lights off for just a minute or two. And there it was. I saw a vehicle matching the descriptions of the getaway car appear about two blocks down the street. It took a left onto Central off of Southwest Boulevard and headed north right toward me. Out of the corner of my eye I saw a police car approaching from the east on Twentieth Street. I had a front-row seat to everything that happened next. As a matter of fact, I was sitting in the crossfire. The cars met in the intersection. The hostage had been forced to drive the car. When he saw the police car, he swerved to the left and stopped right in front of it. The passenger-side door of the getaway car opened, and a guy jumped out. He was holding onto the door and using it as cover. While this was going on, the police officers were getting out of their car. I still remember the officer who got out of the passenger side of the squad car. That's the side that was closest to me.

He took the time to put on his hat, and then both of the officers started toward the getaway car. The officer nearest to me said, "What seems to be the problem?" His question was answered with gunfire. Neither officer had his weapon out when the suspect started shooting. The officer who'd been closest to me went flying back. He had been hit by a bullet. As he flew backward, I saw him pull his revolver and fire it a few times. By this time, his partner was also firing his weapon at the subject. One of them hit the guy, and he went down. I got on my radio and told my dispatcher to get some help. "Officer down," I yelled. All of a sudden there were police cars coming from all directions. They put up tape around the scene and told me I couldn't go anywhere because I had to speak to the detectives. I didn't make any money for the rest of that night.

Come to find out later, the police who were involved in the shooting didn't know anything about the suspect, the robbery, or the hostage. They'd had their radio tuned to a different frequency that night. The next morning it was front page news in the *Kansas City Star* newspaper, and I might add that it was the first time the Kansas City public ever heard the name Richard Tripp. The story in the newspaper was the account I had given to the reporters. The officers involved got the Medal of Valor that year. I, on the other hand, learned a lesson—think twice before looking for adventure.

I learned many lessons during that first year I drove a taxi. I made many friends among the other drivers; many of us became like family. The number one rule we all adhered to was that if you heard a "code blue" go out from any driver, you did whatever it took to cover their back. Code blue meant a driver was in trouble. We were all trained not to mention the word "blue" unless we were in trouble. If you heard the word "blue," it didn't matter if the driver was a friend or an enemy. You responded. All a driver had to say was something like, "There's a blue car in front of me." The dispatcher and the other drivers would know something bad was going on, and every cab in that area would converge on the location of the driver in trouble.

A code blue came over the radio one night when I wasn't very far from the distressed driver. I sped up and headed for his location. Other drivers had heard it too, and they also headed toward the driver. We caught up with him at the corner of Thirty-ninth and Passel. There must have been twenty cabs surrounding that car before the would-be robber knew what hit him, and the majority of drivers had their weapons pointed at the guy. I assure you that it was an intense scene. The guy had a knife to the driver's neck, and the cab couldn't go anywhere because all the other cabs had it surrounded. The would-be robber knew that if he cut the driver, the other drivers on the scene would waste him in a heartbeat.

I jumped out of my cab, walked up to the troubled cab, and said, "Hey, friend, I suggest you throw that knife out the window and let that driver go if you want to see the light tomorrow morning."

I stared straight into his eyes. He looked desperate, and he said, "I'll cut this guy."

"That's your choice," I told him. "But I assure you, you do, and these drivers will unload on you."

After seeing all the guns pointed in his direction, he decided to throw the knife out the window. That's when a couple of the drivers rushed over and dragged him out of the car. It wasn't long before the cops got there and took the guy into custody. By that time, the suspect had been hit a few times, and the drivers had put their guns away. The would-be robber tried to tell the cops that he hadn't tried to rob anybody and that all those drivers had guns.

One of the cops said, "Is that right? I don't see any guns, and I guess if you didn't try to rob that driver, there isn't any reason for us to arrest you. I guess we'll just leave you here with all these drivers."

To which the guy replied, "You can't leave me here with them."

"Well, if there wasn't any crime, then we're not needed," the cop explained.

The guy changed his story real fast and said, "I did try to rob that driver."

We all laughed as the cops hauled the guy off to jail.

You're probably wondering if taxi drivers in Kansas City were allowed to carry guns. The answer is no. We were technically city servants. That meant we were supposed to be sitting targets for the public, but I, as well as many other drivers, preferred to survive on those streets in those taxis. Some of us figured we didn't like being targets. If we wanted to survive, we shot back, right or wrong.

I also know how wild this story sounds, but sometimes the truth is more surprising than fiction, and this incident really did happen. Sometimes when I think back on different incidents that happened during my taxi-driving career, I find that I'm a little remorseful. Then again, when someone is threatening to take your life, your instincts kick in. You figure it's them or you, and you do whatever it takes to survive. Take the call I got one night to pick up a fare at a residence in the ghetto. As I pulled up to the address, I noticed a black man standing on the front porch. He started toward my taxi, and I noticed that though it was dark outside, this guy was wearing sunglasses. To me, that was a red flag, and I started to pull away. That's when I noticed that someone inside the house had started flicking the front porch light on and off. I dropped my guard and backed up. The guy opened the door, and the first thing I saw was the barrel of a gun.

He jumped in the cab and said, "Keep your hands on the wheel and drive."

I drove down the street.

He said, "Pull over here."

I did as I was told.

He said, "When you get stopped, turn the car off."

I pulled over and turned the car off.

He said, "Give me your money."

To say the least, when someone has a gun pointed at you, you're scared. But this guy was scarier because his hand was shaking as he held the gun on me.

I handed over the money as I said, "Hey, I've only got a couple of dollars on me. I just made a money drop at the company."

He started to call me all kinds of names and said, "If you don't give me all your money, I'm going shoot you, honky."

I said, "Well, you're just going to have to shoot me, because them two dollars you got is all I have. Believe me, I wouldn't lie to you with that cannon pointed at me."

He started cussing again. He called me all kinds of things; at the same time, his hand was shaking so badly that in my mind I could see the gun going off. I was really worried that this was where the cops were going find me shot to death.

The guy opened the door and stepped out on the sidewalk, all the while keeping me covered. Then he said, "Start the car and get out of here."

I thought to myself, "With pleasure."

I turned the key, but the car wouldn't start.

He yelled at me, "You dumb, white honky. I said to get."

I tried again, but the car refused to turn over.

I said to him, "Man, I'm trying, but the car won't start."

He continued to cuss at me. And like I said before, I was scared because he kept waving that gun. He started walking down the street behind the car as I frantically tried to get the car to start. It finally started. As I looked in my rearview mirror, I saw the guy turn around and lift his gun like he was going shoot at me.

In a split second I thought to myself, "Screw this."

I threw the car in reverse and backed over him. I might add that I didn't stop to see the damage I'd caused. I didn't really care. What I did do was call 911 from a pay phone. I told the operator that there was a guy lying in the middle of the street, and I gave her the location where I'd left my assailant. I never heard anything else about it. I'm not proud of what I did, but at the time it was him or me. I decided that I didn't have a choice.

At times, it was dangerous on those streets, but there were pleasant moments too. You never knew who you might meet while driving a taxi; you met people you would never meet any other way. That's one of the reasons I kept the job for all these years and still do today. It's really neat when you pick up a celebrity and you're able to brag to your friends about it. Some of the stars I've picked up over the years include Colonel Sanders, Robert De Niro, Lee Greenwood, Tanya Tucker, Loretta Lynn, Evel Knievel, and Mark Victor Hansen. The list goes on and on. There is no other job I can think of that allows a regular Joe to meet and hold a one-on-one conversation with all these people. A taxi driver never knows who's going to jump into their cab.

When I started driving a cab, I was green. But like everyone who makes it through the first year, the job gets in your blood. I think what kept me in the business on and off for thirty years was the excitement of not knowing what might happen next. As added bonuses, you're pretty much your own boss, there is always something new, and being on those streets makes you truly feel like you own the city. Even the cops don't know the territory like a cab driver does.

It takes at least a year to learn where you shouldn't go and where you're going to run into trouble. Once you've got that first year under your belt, you can usually tell when you're in trouble before it happens. You develop a reliable gut feeling, and you learn to read people just by watching them. And when you've driven a cab for as long as I did, you know what to look for. You also learn to talk your way out of trouble before it happens.

If you put in the hours, you can usually make a decent living. You don't get rich, but at least you can eat. If you're single, it's a good job. If you're married, it's a curse, and most married men don't make it. As I stated before, cab drivers put in at least a twelve-hour day. Usually, the days are even longer. There were many days in my past when I worked sixteen to eighteen hours just trying to make a living and feed my family. This gave my dear wife all the time she needed to run around on me. Add the pressures of the job—never knowing if I was going to get shot or robbed—to long hours and a bad marriage, and you can see the situation I was in. The pressure got really bad.

Some might suggest that I should have just found another job, but it wasn't that easy with my health being the way it was. Instead, what I did back then was hit the bottle. If I needed to go to sleep, I'd drink a half pint of whiskey. If I needed to wake up, I'd have a half pint. If I had just been in a shoot-out or robbed, I'd have a half pint. I used the booze like most people used pain pills. It numbed my mind.

How Many Mistakes Can One Man Make?

All of my friends told me I was nuts to want to marry Debby. They all said that she wasn't the marrying kind and would fool around on me like she had in the past. If I'd have been smart, I'd have listened to them. The problem was that I was hardheaded, and I just knew I could change her.

So, against the advice of everyone I knew, including my mother and father, I asked Debby to marry me, and she accepted. I was happy, because I knew the marriage would give me the right to get Joyce Ann out of Debby's stepfather's clutches and I would be able to raise her myself. At least that was my belief at the time. But within a month of our wedding day, we were having problems. It seemed like every other week or so Debby would run home to her stepfather's house. Debby's mother had died, and the only people living at the house were Debby's stepfather, her sisters, and her brothers. One of our problems stemmed from the fact that when Debby was mad at me, she spread a lot of false rumors to her stepfather. This could be one of the reasons he disliked me. She told him that I was never home, I worked too much, I beat her, and that I was a drunk. You name it; she spread it. She spewed all kinds of bullshit, not only to her stepfather but to the rest of her family too. I never knew what rumor she was going start next. During our first five years of marriage, we had three more children: Christina Jean, Rick Jr., and Danny. To tell the complete truth, I *was* working a lot, but it was just to make ends meet.

On more than one occasion, we separated. She would move back to her stepfather's house and start running around with other guys. To tell you the truth, being married to that woman was a living hell. I was in a no-win situation. I got tired of chasing guys away from her. Every time I'd run one off, she would find another. I would have dumped her in a heartbeat if it hadn't been for my children. I think they were the only things that kept me sane.

Of course, by that time, I believe I had become an alcoholic. I wasn't a fall-down drunk. I mainly used alcohol to cope with the insanity I had gotten myself into. Every time Debby and I would have an argument, she would run home to her stepfather, and I found that downright weird. I don't think anything was going on between the two of them, but the situation was really strange. Don't get me wrong, I loved Debby, but I believe she was mentally ill. I'm not sure if she exhibited signs of mental illness when I married her, but the signs were apparent shortly after we got married. This coincided with her mother's death. I'm not trying to make excuses for her behavior, but she became very depressed. As many as five years later, she still had a problem.

Unfortunately, it was about to get worse. I remember waking one night to find her standing above me with a butcher knife in her hand. When I asked her what she was doing, she said, "Mom said to kill you."

Talk about a wake-up call.

I talked her into putting the knife down. I said, "But honey, your mother died a long time ago."

She looked stunned when I said that, and she started crying. After that night, I slept very light if I slept at all. I knew she had a mental problem, and I tried to get her to go see a doctor, but she refused.

It wasn't long after that incident that she approached me and said, "Honey, since you're working so much, I'd like to take the kids and go down south to see my aunt and uncle for a few weeks."

I said, "Well, it might do you and the kids some good to get some country air, but I haven't got the money to send you right now."

She said, "That's okay. I can get the money."

"Oh really? How?" I asked.

"My aunt said she would send me some money, meet me and the kids in Nevada, Missouri, pick us up, and take us to her place. It will be good for the kids to have a place to go swimming. My aunt said they just got a new swimming pool."

I thought about it for a minute and said, "Well, honey, I don't guess it will hurt. When do you plan on going?"

"Next week. I'll call Aunt Rita and tell her to send the money."

Debby spent the next week acting like everything was fine. I never thought there was anything wrong when I put her and the kids on that Greyhound bus headed for Nevada. I gave all the kids kisses and hugs; then I gave her one and said, "I'll call you tonight, honey."

"Okay, Rick, I love you."

The bus took off with my family, and I went back to work thinking everything was fine. What I eventually learned much later from one of her relatives was that her aunt hadn't sent her the money for the tickets. A battered women's shelter had given her the tickets after she'd told them she was afraid I was going to hurt her and the kids. She'd apparently told them that I was drunk all the time and beat her up. Who knows what else she told them.

I talked to her several times on the phone that week, and everything seemed to be going fine. It must have been about a week later when I called and her aunt said, "She doesn't want to talk to you."

"What the hell do you mean, she doesn't want to talk to me?"

Her aunt hung up the phone. I tried back several times, and each time they hung up on me. I couldn't figure out what was going on. Why in the hell had both Debby and her aunt suddenly stopped talking to me? I must have called down there a hundred times that week. A few days later some light was shed on the situation when divorce papers were served to me at my home.

I immediately placed a call to Debby. Her Uncle Ben, answered the phone.

I said, "This is Rick. I just got these damn divorce papers served on me. Let me talk to Debby."

She got on the phone, and I asked her, "What in the hell is going on down there, Debby?"

She said, "Do I have to paint you a picture? I don't love you anymore."

"Oh really," I replied. "Where in the hell are my kids?"

"They're with my cousin up at the park."

"You had this planned all along, before you even went down there. Didn't you?"

"Well, no. It just happened. I've got to go, Rick."

"What in the hell do you mean, you've got to go?"

"My friends are waiting for me."

"What friends?" I yelled.

"Nobody you know."

"Well, I tell you what. I'll be down there this weekend, and I'll meet your damn friends then. What do you think about that?"

"My uncle and aunt don't want you down here," she said.

"I don't care what any of those hillbillies want," I yelled. "I'm going to come down and have a talk with you about these divorce papers, and I'm going to see my kids."

About that time, Debby's Uncle Ben, got on the phone and said, "Rick, Debby doesn't want you down here. As a matter of fact, my wife and I don't want you here either. We had Debby file a protection order on you along with the divorce papers. If you come anywhere near my property, you'll be going to jail."

Those were his last words as he hung up the phone. I tried to call him back to tell him off, but nobody would answer. I was pissed. Who in the hell did he think he was talking to? He was lucky he wasn't near me when he made that statement. I'd have whipped his butt.

I had a drink and started thinking. The only difference between this incident and the others Debby had pulled was the divorce papers. It definitely wasn't the first time she had run off to stay with her family and told them how bad I was, and it wasn't the first time she had gotten a protection order on me. About the only difference was that this time she had left town. I started to think it would just be a matter of time before her relatives realized that she had a screw loose. They would get tired of her or she would get tired of them, and she'd head back home with the kids.

I decided that the best thing I could do was just sit back and wait. It wouldn't do me any good to run down there and take a chance on going to jail. I knew the odds were that sooner or later she would show back up at my door. So, for a few months I did just that. I sat back and waited for her to show up at my door. I'd call down, talk to her, ask about the kids, and ask her if she was tired of it down there yet. What I didn't know was that she'd been dating a guy down there the entire time she'd been gone. Along with her relatives, this guy helped her apply for and receive a monthly check from the welfare department. He also found her a house to rent in Nevada.

The day came when I called her aunt and uncle's house and her uncle told me, "She doesn't live here anymore."

It caught me off guard.

"Well, where in the hell does she live, and where in the hell are my kids?"

"In Nevada," he replied. "The kids started back to school last week."

"Well, has she got a phone where I can call her?"

"I don't really know," he replied.

I hung up and called directory assistance for Nevada, Missouri. I got her number, called it, and a guy answered the phone.

I said, "Is this Debby Tripp's phone number?"

"Yes, it is. Who is this?" the voice asked.

"This is her husband. Who in the hell is this?"

"She doesn't want to talk to you," the voice said before hanging up.

I called back and told the creep who answered the phone, "You hang up on me again, and I'll come down there and find you, and when I do, you'll wish you were never born."

The voice replied, "You don't even know who I am, and besides that, I'm not scared of you. Make the mistake of coming to my town, and me and my friends will wash you off our streets." With that, he hung up again.

He was right. I didn't know who he was, but I was going find out, and then maybe I'd pay him a visit when he least expected it. We'd find out if he was as bad as he thought he was.

Because my plan to sit back and wait for Debby to return with the kids didn't seem to be working, I decided that it might be time to use my ace in the hole. The next day I went to work, where I ran into Jeff, another taxi driver who over the years had become a good friend of mine. Jeff was my ace in the hole. He was married to one of Debby's cousins, and he had the inside track into the goings-on in Nevada, Missouri. Better yet, Debby's family thought Jeff and I were enemies, because we always acted like we didn't like each other when we were around them. What they didn't know was that we had been friends before I met Debby, before he'd met his wife, and before either of us had met Debby's family.

I told Jeff about the guy answering the phone at Debby's house and asked him to keep his ears open and see what he could find out for me.

He said, "No problem, Bro. I'll find out who he is and where he hangs out."

"Okay, thanks. Let me know what you learn," I said.

Jeff did find out who the guy was and where he liked to hang out, and it was on my agenda to go have it out with him. However, fate had other plans for the guy. It seems he was out drinking one night when he missed a curve on a country road and had an accident and killed himself. I never did get to have a face-to-face with the guy.

A week or so later, I got the final divorce decree. It stated that Debby and I were divorced and that she had been granted custody of the kids. I knew it was coming, but I had thought she would come back home after her boyfriend died. I can remember reading the decree, picking up a bottle of booze, and remaining drunk for a week or so before I went back to work.

During the next few months, all I did was work, pay the bills, get drunk, and chase women. I was 35 years old and again alone. My second wife had followed in my first wife's footsteps, taking my kids and running away. During that time, I harbored an ache in my heart for the four children I now had living down in Nevada, Missouri, not to mention the two children that I had with Becky. I hadn't seen Dawn and Keith since before I'd married Debby. I felt like a complete loser.

Then my phone rang. It was Debby.

"Rick, me and the kids need a favor."

"What do you need?"

"We need a place to stay in Kansas City. I've got to come up there and have a hysterectomy, and I won't be able to do any work for six weeks while I'm recuperating."

"Well, if it's that important, then come on up. When are you having the operation?"

"Next week," she replied.

"Okay, I'll pick you guys up at the Greyhound station Friday night."

When I put that phone down, I thought I had won. I thought I was going to have my babies back that next week. It didn't turn out that way though. When Debby got off the bus, she was alone.

"Where in the hell are the kids?" I asked.

"I left them with my aunt. I didn't figure you would have a way of watching them while I was tied down for six weeks."

At first I was pissed. Basically, she was using me. After a while, I figured out that if I treated her nice, we could drive down and get the kids after she'd recuperated. Once that happened, there was no way I'd ever let them out of my sight again. I would talk Debby into getting married again just to make sure my plan worked.

About a week after she had the operation, she got a phone call from the Vernon County Welfare Office. They had tracked her down through her aunt, and the aunt had given the welfare office my phone number. A representative from the welfare office told Debby that they had custody of my children and were going to charge her with child abandonment. She told them that she had just had an operation and she couldn't even move. She told them that she would come to their office to speak with them when she was mobile.

When she got off the phone, I asked, "What in the hell is going on? Why in the hell does the Department of Family Services have custody of my children?"

"I don't know, Rick."

"I don't know either, Debby, but I'll bet you I find out. Give me that phone. I'm going to call them and find out what in the hell is going on."

"Wait a minute, Rick. I've got something to tell you." She was crying, but she continued, "You know I told you my aunt was watching the kids?"

"Yes, what about it?"

"Well, that wasn't really true."

"Well, then, where have they been all this time?"

"I had a girlfriend down there. She lived next to me, and she was supposed to be babysitting them for me."

"Well, if that's the case, how in the hell did DFS get involved?"

"I don't know, Rick."

"Well, I'm going find out."

I called the DFS office and asked them about my children. I was told, "Mr. Tripp, we can't speak to you about the case or the welfare of the children because of the law. You're not the custodial parent of the children."

"Look lady, I've got their mother lying right here in a bed, and she can't move because she has to stay in bed for six weeks."

"Well Mr. Tripp, when she can move, tell her to get a hold of us, and we'll discuss the children with her. Until then, a judge has placed them in the Department of Family Services' custody as wards of the court."

"Well, lady, I just got one more question for you," I said.

"I'll answer it for you if I can, Mr. Tripp."

"How did you guys decide my kids were abandoned? My ex-wife claims she paid someone to watch them."

"All I can tell you is that a hotline was called, and we sent a caseworker to check it out. That's when the children were taken into our custody."

"Okay, thank you," I said, before hanging up the phone.

I was so angry when I got off the phone that I started cussing out Debby and her family. I was saying things like, "You dumb bitch, and how could you pull this shit and lose my babies?" I added some garbage about how I would kick the asses of her entire family if they ever got in my way again. In other words, I was acting like a complete idiot. Basically, my temper was out of control for the rest of that evening. I started drinking to try to calm myself down, and I guess it worked, because I finally passed out.

Fast-forward six weeks. Debby was preparing to return to Nevada to face her DFS worker. The plan was to get the kids back, and I thought we had a good chance of doing so. She still had her house in Nevada, which would work to her benefit in regaining custody of the kids. I had devised a plan that included getting the kids back, getting remarried, and starting over. I thought everything was worked out between us. But once Debby spoke to the caseworker, all the plans I had worked out with her were void. She told them so many lies about me that the DFS workers didn't even want me to see the kids without supervision. Between the lies she told and the way I'd treated the caseworkers, I guess they decided I was unfit. But the real kicker hadn't happened yet. I had to set up a meeting with Debby's DFS caseworker before I could see my children. At the meeting, I was informed that I would have to start giving DFS money to support my children. I didn't really see anything wrong with that, and I was ready to turn over some money. However, I wasn't happy to learn that I could only see my children under DFS supervision and the visits would have to take place at their office in Nevada, but I figured I could eventually get a lawyer and have those arrangements altered.

I asked the caseworker, "So, when can I see my children?"

"Well, we can make arrangements for you to start seeing the boys here next week," she said.

"Well, that's fine. What about my girls? Will I see them at the same time?"

"Well, Mr. Tripp, according to our records and what your ex-wife has told us, the girls are not your daughters. As a matter of fact, I believe they have the last name of Gunn, not Tripp. That's according to their birth certificates, and that's what we go by."

I know I didn't do my case any good at that meeting, because I blew my cool and started yelling at the caseworker.

"Are you nuts? I don't care what name is on those birth certificates, you crazy bitch. Everybody knows those are my babies, and I'll tell you something else, you won't get a damn cent from me until I see all my kids—my boys *and* my girls. I'm not going to put mental baggage on my kids by having them think I love only some of them and not the others. You got that straight, lady?"

"Mr. Tripp, this meeting is over."

"You're damn right it is," I yelled as I stormed out of the office.

I was so hot. If they would have said another word to me, I'm pretty sure I would have popped one of them and ended up in the county jail. I jumped in my car and headed back to Kansas City. Of course, I stopped for a drink on the way.

I knew then that my plans to reconcile with Debby were dead. I never wanted to have anything to do with her ever again. In fact, if I'd have seen her after that meeting, I'm sure I'd still be in prison. I eventually lost track of Debby, not that I gave a damn. But the thing that bugged me most is having the feeling that Debby really didn't seem to want the kids? She just didn't want me to have them and I might add she never did get back custody of them.

For years after that meeting I tried everything I could think of to get to see my kids. But DFS was always there throwing up roadblocks. They did everything they could to keep me from seeing my girls. They did, however, let me see the boys once in awhile. I even went to court a couple of times to try to get custody of them, but DFS would tell the judge that it would be best if the kids stayed in the system. They said I was a taxi driver, and I wasn't home much. I told the judge that I could hire a nanny while I was working. He said that plan didn't sound feasible and that minor children needed more supervision than that. He added that because I lived in Jackson County, he didn't feel right about turning the children loose with me and letting me take them to another jurisdiction where his county's DFS department had no control of the outcome.

I argued that Jackson County also had a DFS division, but I still lost the battle to get custody of my children.

I knew right then that getting my children out of Vernon County Department of Family Services custody was going to take a miracle, a lot of money, and a top-notch lawyer. I might add that I didn't have any of these resources. I did, however, make one more attempt on my own to have the children released to me. Before that hearing, I saw Debby, who was also trying to get custody of the kids, and her DFS caseworker walking down the street together. They were talking and smiling like they were the best of friends. When the caseworker headed into the courthouse where the hearing was to be held, Debby gave her a hug. I then turned to enter the courthouse, while Debby jumped into a car and left with some guy I had never seen before. I thought that was strange. Because she was also seeking custody of the kids, I had expected her to be at this hearing. At the time, I had no idea just how far she and that caseworker would go or how many lies they would tell to keep me from getting custody of my children. It didn't take long to find out. In the middle of the hearing, the caseworker told the judge that there had been some new developments in the case of the Tripp minor children.

"What are they?" he asked the caseworker.

"Well, Judge, it's been brought to my attention that Mr. Tripp might have been molesting the girls, Joyce and Christina."

I couldn't believe what I had just heard, and before I knew it, I opened my mouth and said something like, "You are a crazy lady."

The judge said, "That will be enough of that, Mr. Tripp."

I said, "I'm sorry, Judge, but I can't believe she just said that."

He looked back in her direction and said, "Do you have any proof to substantiate that the children were molested?"

"Not at this time, Your Honor."

"Have you had the children in question checked by a doctor?"

"Yes, Judge, but the tests came back inconclusive. We have launched an investigation into the allegations, and we have appointments set up for the girls to start seeing a child psychiatrist. It could take a while to complete the investigation. For the welfare of the children, we believe these custody proceedings should only continue after we finish our investigation."

When the caseworker was done speaking, the judge looked at me and said, "And what do you think, Mr. Tripp?"

"Judge, I think this is just another delay by that caseworker and my ex-wife to keep me from getting custody of my children. Anyone who knows me wouldn't believe that I would have anything to do with my children sexually. To me, Your Honor, a person that messes with kids in the first place ought to be shot, but if I was guilty of what they are trying to say about me, I assure you that I would kill myself. I can't think of anything worse than a child molester." I paused, then said, "I take that back, Judge, there is something worse. What's worse is what DFS is trying to do here today. They're spreading lies and allegations about me without having to prove anything. Regardless of what you decide today, when they get done with their investigation, I want to know where these accusations started."

The judge ruled that day to delay me getting custody of my kids. DFS conducted their investigation, and naturally, I was cleared. But word got out that DFS had accused me of being a child molester, and even though nothing was proven, the rumors spread like wildfire. Unfortunately, caseworkers can spread any rumor they want. According to the state of Missouri, they don't have to prove anything, and you can't sue them.

I was finally able to start seeing my boys, but I wasn't able to see my daughters until they turned 18 and out of the system. Many years later, when I finally got to see them, they told me stories about how they had been treated by their foster families, and some of these stories were gruesome. I heard stories from both my girls and my boys. They told tales of everything from being sexually molested to one of my sons having his jaw broken by a staff member at Boys Town, the center he'd been placed in.

Of course, I didn't find out about any of these abuses until after my children were out of the system. Those Vernon County Department of Family Services caseworkers even tried to keep the records of my children's incarceration in the states welfare system from them. Each of my children was forced to sign a waiver or a release of some type before they were allowed to see their records before they left the system. The release stated something along the lines that DFS wasn't liable for anything that had happened to them while they were wards of the state.

Naturally, their stories filled me with rage, but there wasn't anything I could do about it. By then, my children were grown. All I could do was try to make it up to them. I tried to let them know that regardless of what had transpired while they were in the custody of the state of Missouri, I loved each and every one of them. I told them that I had thought about each of them every single day, no matter what they had been told by their caseworkers or the various foster families they had been assigned to over the years. According to my children, plenty had been said about me. Unlike back then, today I speak to all my kids almost daily. Each of my children has blessed me with grandchildren, and their grandpa tries to see each of them as often as possible. God has even blessed me with a great-granddaughter, and a great-grandson is on the way.

I'd like to blame all my problems on the system that was in place at that time, my ex-wives, their families, and the Missouri Department of Family Services. I'd love to be able to tell everyone that the bad things that happened to my children were through no fault of my own. But the truth is that if I would have left the bottle alone and used my head more, my kids might not have had to go through hell. I just hope that one day they can truly forgive me for the mistakes I made, and I hope they understand that although their father did become an alcoholic while they were growing up, it wasn't because he didn't care about them.

Losing my children was actually one of the reasons I turned to alcohol. After years of making the wrong choices, the guilt, the pain, and the alcohol addiction associated with both turned me into a ship without a rudder. I'd become a person who tried to drown all of life's unpleasantness in a bottle rather than the young man who had once thought he could take on the world. That once fearless man had become a shell of a man who was defeated, weathered, bruised, torn, and helpless. At times, I didn't even understand why I was still alive. As a matter of fact, there were times when I longed for death because the pain in my soul was so great. My enemies had figured out that my weakness was my children. With my vulnerability exposed, I had let the world chew me up and spit me out. With the help of alcohol, I had let myself go so low that the fight wasn't in me anymore. On the outside, I probably looked the same to most people, but on the inside, my spirit resembled that of a dead man. It went on that way for years, until I ended up homeless. That's when God gave me a new mission.

Needless to say, Debby never did regain custody of our four children. I had thought she was a shoo-in for custody after the way she and her caseworker had carried on like old friends the day of my hearing. It's speculation on my part, but I've always assumed DFS figured out that she had some mental problems. I do know that a year or so later, I got a call one morning from my friend Jeff. He was my fellow taxi driver who had been married to Joy, Debby's cousin. He told me that he and his wife, Joy, were breaking up, and she was shacking up with some guy here in the city. He said his wife had told him that Debby and my children were visiting Joy. He then said, "I'm going over to see my kids tonight. Why don't you come with me and see yours?"

I thought about it for a minute before I said, "Hey, Jeff, something doesn't sound right about that. The last I heard, the state still had custody of my kids. I haven't heard anything about the kids being returned to Debby."

"Well, Tripp, that's what Joy, said."

"Well, if they are there tonight, call me and I'll come over. But personally I think it's bullshit."

I didn't get a call that evening, but the next morning when I turned the television on, I did get a shock. The news announcer said that on the previous night, two brothers had been shot at a residence on the east side of town. One of the men—it turned out to be Jeff—was dead, and the bullet that killed him had also hit his brother Brett. After the newscast was over, I went to Truman Medical Center. That's where the news announcer said the brothers had been taken for treatment. I wanted to talk to Jeff's brother, Brett, to find out what had happened. To this day I don't know if Brett was lying to me or not, but the story he told me was different from what the police told me later. Brett said that he and Jeff set off to visit Jeff's kids at the residence of the man Joy was shacking up with. Without warning, as they pulled into the driveway, a guy jumped out of the bushes and shot Jeff with a .30-30 deer rifle. He was about to shoot again when Joy ran out of the house and yelled, "That's his brother; that's not Tripp."

According to Brett, that kept the guy from firing off another round. The bullet that hit Jeff in the head also went into Brett's side. When I left Brett's hospital room, I was mad as hell. I called the police department and asked to speak to the detective in charge of the shooting. I said that I had some information that might have something to do with the case. They told me to come down to the police station to be interviewed. During the interview, I told the detective about the call I had gotten from Jeff the day before, and I told him the story Brett had told me.

The detective said, "I don't think it went down the way his brother Brett told you, Mr. Tripp, and we're charging the living brother with trespassing."

"Well, what about the guy who shot Jeff? What are you charging him with?"

"We're not; we consider the incident a justifiable homicide. I'm sorry, Mr. Tripp, but everything points to Jeff and his brother going on the man's property to do harm to the gentleman. The shooter was just protecting his property."

"You're going let that son of a bitch get away with murder?"

"I know you're upset, Mr. Tripp, but those brothers were on private property."

I knew right then that Joy's boyfriend was going to get away with killing Jeff. I was also aware that if our paths ever crossed, I would avenge the killing. Whether it was a setup or not, whether Brett had lied to me or not, the point was that this man had killed a good friend of mine. If Brett was telling the truth, then Joy's boyfriend had been prepared to shoot me too. Whether Debby's family had tried to get both of us at one time or not, I wouldn't have given them another chance. If nothing else, Jeff's death kept me from ever wanting to get involved with Debby or her family again.

Rehabilitation

Month's after being admitted to the hospital the doctor came in one morning after I'd been admitted to the hospital for vomiting blood. She asked, "Mr. Tripp, how are you feeling this morning?"

Because there was a tube down my throat, I had to communicate via the written word. I wrote, "Okay, I guess."

"Well, we're going to move you later today. We're sending you to Truman East out in Lee's Summit for rehabilitation. We have done everything we can for you here. The ambulance will be here this afternoon to transport you. This will be the last time I'll be acting as your doctor. You'll get a new team of doctors over there."

On the tablet I wrote, "Thank you for all your help."

She smiled and said, "Just remember what I said about the drinking." With that she left. I remembered very will what she had told me about the drinking? When I had come to 38 days after I arrived in the hospital she had come in and had a special little talk with me about my drinking, She had warned me that if I ended back up in her emergency room, and I had the smell of alcohol on me, the next time I woke up out of a coma I might have body parts were they shouldn't ought to be. She explained to me that a blood vessel in my throat had burst and that is what started me bleeding, and that it was a miracle I was still alive, because the majority of people that had that condition died before they could get the bleeding to stop. The reason they had kept me in a drug induced coma for the first 38 days of that hospital stay was to give me a better chance of making it.

She also made the statement, "I don't know why God let you live through that bleed, but he must have something special for you to do in your life time."

I also think she was trying to scare me in a sense about drinking. And I can honestly say she scared me and I haven't had a drink since I was 45. I am 59 now, so that means for the past 14 years I have been sober. Also COPP didn't really start getting known until after I stopped drinking.

A few hours after lunch, the nurses came in and started packing up my belongings. One of the nurses said, "We have to get you into another bed for transport, Mr. Tripp."

I was still hooked to IVs, breathing tubes, and who knows what else. They were going to have to move me and a lot of gear. During the move downstairs to the ambulance, the nurse who was in charge of transporting me to the ambulance had to wait for the elevator to stop on our floor. She left me there by the elevator for a minute or two while she attended to another patient. As I sat there, my respirator malfunctioned. It wasn't working properly, and I wasn't getting the airflow I needed. I started freaking out. I thought I was going to die right there. I tried to talk, but couldn't because there was a mask on my face. I also couldn't see the nurses from my vantage point. Thankfully, she was nearby. She could see me trying to sit up, rushed back over to check on me, and quickly figured out I wasn't getting enough air. She pulled my mask off and stuck another one on me. This one was hooked to a tank, and I started breathing normally.

The nurse said, "Sorry about that, Mr. Tripp."

I was just thankful she had seen me trying to get up.

After that, everything about the trip to Truman East went fine. The next morning, I met the new team of doctors. The first thing they said after they checked me out was, "We're going to start getting you ready so you can go home in a few weeks. Tomorrow we're going take the tube out of your throat so you can talk."

I wrote, "Thank you, Doc. It's about time."

The next morning, that's exactly what they did. I was so happy to get my voice back that I started calling all my relatives on the phone. That afternoon, my mother and sister showed up during afternoon visiting hours. We had a good chat until the afternoon visiting hours were over. That night my daughter, Dawn Kay, showed up. I was never so happy to see anybody in my life as when my baby girl, that wasn't a baby anymore and in her late twenties, walked into that hospital room.

The reason I'd been transferred to Truman Medical Center East was so I could start my rehabilitation. The hospital was expecting its rehab staff to be able to get me out of that bed and get me walking again. I needed to build up the muscles in my legs along with other parts of my body. Several members of their rehab staff encouraged me to go to their rehab center every day to work out. The problem was that every time I tried to sit up or get out of bed, my blood pressure would drop, and I would almost pass out. I guess it was from all those months I hadn't been on my feet. I would tell those on the rehab staff that I couldn't get up.

It took fear and shock to get me out of that bed. One day while my mother was there visiting, the doctor came into my room and said, "Mrs. Fields, it looks like we're going have to put your son in a nursing home."

That statement got my attention.

I asked, "What did you say, Doc?"

He repeated his line about the nursing home.

I asked, "Are you joking? You've got to be out of your mind. I'm only forty-five. You're not putting me in any damn nursing home."

"Well, we can't get you to get out of that bed, so we have no choice."

As soon as he'd threatened me with a nursing home, I decided that I'd do whatever it took to get out of that bed. I guess he knew how to pull my strings. By the end of that week, I was walking unassisted.

Before I'd ended up in the hospital, I'd been living at the hotel on Seventy-Seventh and Prospect, and everything I owned had been in the old car I'd been driving. I didn't have much, but everything I did have, including my clothes, had been in that car. While I was in the hospital, it had been stolen from the hotel parking lot. So I didn't even have a change of clothes. The ones I had worn to the hospital had been cut off of me. Thankfully, my sister had gone out and bought me some shirts and pants, but there was still a problem. I couldn't be released from the hospital unless I had somewhere to go, and all those doctors could think of was having the state of Missouri put me in a nursing home. They said I was in too bad a shape to be on my own. They didn't think I'd be able to take care of myself.

By that time, my mother had moved out of town. She was living back with my stepfather, in Versailles, Missouri and they were planning to remarry. But she still owned her home in Blue Springs. It was only about ten minutes from the hospital. The problem was that even if I stayed there, I would need someone to watch me. She told me not to worry; she said she would think of something, and she did. She talked my little brother, his wife, and their kids into moving back up to her house from their home in Versailles, Missouri to watch me until I could get better. They would stay there with me during the week and get me to the hospital when I needed to go. My mother and stepfather would come up on the weekends to give them a break. Although my little brother, Darrell, was my half brother, we still had a good relationship. As a matter of fact, I had changed his diapers when he was little. Thank God, Darrell and his wife agreed, or I just might have ended up in a nursing home. There aren't too many brothers or friends who would just pack up and move to another city to help a relative or a friend.

I was released from the hospital and started living at my mom's house in Blue Springs. I was there about two weeks when the unthinkable happened. I was staying in my mother's master bedroom. It was on a weekend when my mom and my stepfather were there serving as caretakers. I awoke sick and vomiting at about two in the morning. I tried to yell for my mother, but they had a fan on in the front room. So I lay there for a few hours, trying to yell at them. I guess my blood pressure was low, because I could hardly speak by the time they heard me.

My mother came in, saw the condition I was in, and said, "Hank, call an ambulance."

By the time the paramedics arrived, they could hardly find a pulse. They rushed me to the hospital and started doing the same things again; I was stuck with needles and the whole smear. My veins were collapsing, so they ended up putting the IV in my jugular vein. Apparently I'd been vomiting dried blood. Hospital personnel decided that I should be admitted for a few more weeks. They wanted to make sure the bleeding wouldn't start again. They never did really figure out what caused that bout of bleeding. They thought it might have been the acid in some fresh tomatoes I'd been eating, but that was just a theory.

By the time I was discharged this time around, my strength had already started to return. This was unlike my previous stay. With the help of a cane, I had started to actually get around better. I started walking farther and farther. When they dismissed me from the hospital, I returned to my mother's place, but this time around I didn't need as much supervision. I could get out of bed, go to the bathroom, take a shower, and that kind of stuff.

While I'd been in the hospital, my daughter Dawn had come out to see me quite a bit. She had said, "Dad, if you get tired of staying at Grandma's, you can always come stay with me at my place."

I gave that a lot of thought over the next few weeks and finally decided that taking her up on her offer might be just the thing to do. It helped that I knew my brother and sister-in-law were missing their home down in Versailles. So the next weekend, when my mother and stepfather showed up, I told them that I had decided to move in with my daughter.

My mother said, "Are you sure you want to do that, Son?"

"Well, Mom, Darrell and Tracy have their own life to live, and I know they're missing Versailles. Before, I couldn't get around, but now I can; and besides that, I want to get back to town, where I can see friends and maybe get back to work."

"Don't rush it, Rick. You're not in that good of shape yet."

"I know, Mom, but I will be before long."

"Okay, Son, if that's what you want to do."

So that next week, I moved back to Kansas City with my daughter Dawn.

Before I left my mother's house, I thanked my little brother and his wife for all the help they had given me. They said, "Rick, we can stay here if you don't really want to leave. We don't mind."

"That's okay, Darrell, you have your own life to live. I'm sure your kids will be happy to move back home and see their friends," I said.

I had my mother drop me off at my daughter's house. Before pulling away, she said, "Son, if you need me, I'm just a phone call away."

My daughter spoke up, "Don't worry, Grandma. I'll take good care of him." And with that, my mother gave me a hug and headed back to Versailles.

Something Is Coming

I looked out the window of my daughter's house to make sure my cab was still there. You might say I was just making sure that I wasn't dreaming about picking it up from the owners the night before. It was there. I still wasn't feeling very well, but I felt better knowing that the cab was sitting out there. Have you ever seen the scene in the movie *West Side Story* where Tony and the storekeeper are talking and Tony reveals that he doesn't know where or what, but he feels something coming? Well, that is how I was feeling, lying there on my daughter's divan, looking out the window at that cab. Although I was terribly weak, something was telling me to get up and get going. I didn't really know why, but I knew it was the thing to do.

The night before, I had pulled off the con of my life getting the owners to relinquish their cab to me. With the help of a cane, I had walked as straight as I could, in an effort to convince them that they should give me the cab. If they had seen how weak I had really been, they would have never turned me loose with it. I reached over, grabbed the walker the hospital had given me, pulled myself up, walked over to my clothes, and began to get dressed. It took me quite a while, but I got the job done. Getting the pants on was the hardest. I had to hold onto the walker with one hand while putting my pants on with the other. I had to sit in a chair to put my shirt on. Making just that small effort zapped my energy.

I yelled for Dawn. She was in her bedroom asleep.

"Hey, Dawn," I repeated.

She woke up. "What you need, Dad?" she asked.

"I can't find the coffee; could you please find it for me?"

She got up and walked into the kitchen. "What time is it, Dad?" she asked.

I said, "I guess it's about six o'clock."

"What are you doing up at this time of morning?" she asked.

"I'm going to work," I replied.

She looked over at me and said, "You're not serious, are you?"

"Yep."

"But Dad, you're not in any condition to go to work. I watched you come in from that car last night, and I thought you were going to fall on your face."

"I'll be okay," I assured her.

"But Dad, you might get in a wreck or hurt somebody if you go out. I sure don't understand why those people turned you loose with their car," she said as she walked into the kitchen, shaking her head.

A few minutes later, she returned with a cup of coffee. She had a worried and concerned look on her face.

"Look," I said as I grabbed her hand, "I was driving before you were born, and I'm just as good a driver now as I was then."

"But you just got out of the hospital, and I know you're taking that medicine. It might make you sleepy, or you could pass out or something."

I looked in her eyes and said, "Now, don't worry. I'll be okay. If I get sleepy, I'll come home."

"But …"

I cut her off. "Dawn, I can't take another day of just lying on that divan. I've got to get back to work, but I'll take it easy. I promise."

She looked at me with a lot of doubt in her eyes, and as she walked away she said, "Okay, Dad, but if you have any problems, you call me."

I assured her that I would, and she went back to bed. I sat there alone for a while and drank my coffee. The problem was that I had assured her I was fine, but in my own mind I knew that the walk out the door and to the cab would be a long one because I was feeling very weak. However, I also had a feeling that it had to be done.

I finished my coffee, grabbed a hold of the walker, and headed for the door. The journey from the front door to the cab was only about twenty feet, but that morning it felt like it was twenty miles. By the time I got to the cab, I was as weak as could be, but I kept pushing myself one step at a time until I'd reached the trunk of the cab. I inserted the key into the truck lock and opened the trunk with one hand as I kept my other hand on the walker. With my free hand, I then grabbed the side of the car. With the hand I'd been keeping on the walker, I folded the contraption, put it in the trunk, and shut the lid. I kept a hold of the car, slid around to the front door, stuck the key in the door lock, and turned it. I almost fell as I opened the door. Instead, I was able to grab the top of the door and slide myself into the driver's seat. I sat there in that seat for a good five minutes or so before I reached over to grab the door, retrieve the key, and insert it in the ignition. I sat still for at least another five minutes before I tried to start the car.

I adjusted the mirror and hit the button to move the front seat into the right position. The night before I had driven it home, but hadn't really adjusted the seats or mirror to where they needed to be to drive it comfortably. I was lucky the car had power seats, because I don't think I had the strength to reach under the seat to make the adjustment. About now, had you seen me, you may have been compelled to ask me what the heck I was doing in the front seat of that car. Some might have even said I was an accident looking to happen. Looking back now, both statements were warranted, but at the time, I had a burning desire to be in that cab.

Something was coming. I didn't know what it was, but I knew that getting in that cab that day would be a turning point in my life. I don't know how I knew, but I knew. As it turned out—call it a premonition, call it luck, or call it fate—I ended up being one hundred percent right.

I started the car, put it in drive, and headed downtown. It felt good being back behind the wheel after spending so much time in the hospital. It actually felt better than good. You might say that I felt as if I was once again in control of my life.

I jumped on the freeway and opened up the car's engine. Before being converted into a cab, that particular car had been a state patrol car. It ran like the wind, and it only took a few seconds to get it up to seventy miles an hour. The next exit was the one I wanted, so I slowed down. Damn, it felt good having the wind blow through my hair. It had been a long time since I had experienced that feeling. I almost felt human again.

When I had been in that hospital, I couldn't control anything. But here in this car, one might say that I was again in my element. It didn't take long for me and the car to become one, so to speak. I just felt so alive.

I headed for a hotel to find a fare. I drove by several of them, but the cabstands were all full of cabs. I decided to head for the Crown Center Complex. It consisted of two hotels: the Crown Center Hotel and the Hyatt Regency Hotel. The cabstand at the Crown was full of cabs, so I went around the block to the Hyatt where the cabstand was empty. I pulled up on the stand and turned my motor off. This cabstand was different from others of its time. This cabstand was a full block from the hotel's entrance. A pole with a light on top had been installed at the cabstand for the Hyatt. When the hotel needed a taxi, the light on the pole would flash. This is how you knew you could drive on up and retrieve your fare.

I'd been sitting on the stand for just a few minutes when the light started flashing. I drove up to the driveway, and the doorman motioned for me to pull off to the side and open my trunk. "I have a guy going to the airport," he said. I pulled over and pushed the button that opened my trunk. The doorman stuck a couple of bags in the trunk, shut the lid, and told me that the fare would be out in a minute or two. It looked like this just might be my lucky day. When driving a cab, the fare you really want to get takes you to the airport. These are the fares that pay the most money. And here, my first fare out of the hospital wanted to go to the airport. That was a good omen, if ever I saw one.

Anyway, I looked toward the bellman and out walked this guy. He chitchatted with the bellman before handing him some money. The bellman pointed the guy toward my car, walked him over, opened the back door for him, and said, "Have a great day, Mr. Hansen. Come back to see us soon, sir."

The guy got in the cab and said, "Airport, Cabbie."

I replied "Yes, sir."

You can read about the trip in Mr. Hansen's own book, *A Cup of Chicken Soup for the Soul.* From my viewpoint, there seemed to be something very special about this man. The first time I saw him talking to that bellman, I knew there was something special about him. For one thing, you could tell by the way he was dressed. He was dressed in a suit, but it wasn't an ordinary, run-of-the-mill businessman's suit. It was tailored to fit him to a T. I also noticed his cufflinks and the fact that his initials were hand sewn into the cuffs of his sleeves. My passenger was obviously one very classy act. Even his shoes were outstanding. I had never seen a pair of shoes that color, but they perfectly matched the suit he was wearing.

As we pulled out onto the street, I asked him, "Where are you flying off to?"

"LA," he replied.

As I looked at him in the rearview mirror, the next thing I asked was, "Were you in town for business or pleasure?"

"I had to give a talk to the Re/Max Realtors convention," he replied.

"Oh really? What did you speak about?"

"My new book I have out, *Chicken Soup for the Soul.*"

"You're a writer?"

"Yep, among other things. Have you heard of my book?"

"No, sir, I can't really say I have, but then again, I don't read very much. I stay too busy to read much."

"Oh really," he said. "What do you do? Do you drive a lot, or what?"

"Well, to tell you the truth, I do drive a lot, but I also run a program to help the homeless and poor here in Kansas City. I do that when I can. You see, I just got out of the hospital. As a matter of fact, you're my first passenger since I got out."

"What was wrong with you?" he asked.

"Well, I had a bleed, and I was in the hospital for about nine months."

"Sorry to hear that. Are you okay now?" he asked.

"I guess I am. Only time will tell."

Throughout our conversation, I watched his facial expressions in the rearview mirror. He was a nice enough guy, but I could tell that he may have been feeling a little apprehensive about my health.

If he had only known, he just might have caught a different cab. But he was in my taxi now, and I wasn't going to let someone else get the fare.

The next thing he wanted to know was which program I ran for the poor and homeless of Kansas City.

"We take care of ten thousand or so poor and homeless brothers and sisters on Christmas morning, kids and all, by providing them with Christmas breakfast and giving them materials to survive on the streets during the winter."

"Very commendable," he said.

"Well, somebody has to do it," I said.

About that time we'd approached Ninth Street. I told him to look over at the building on the left, which is where my charitable office was located. There was a sign in the window that read "Care of Poor People."

We continued northbound and came across the Broadway Bridge, where I had lived for a year while I had been homeless. I pointed the area out to him and told him how I had learned to survive on the streets.

About that time, I said, "Enough about me. How about you tell me something about yourself?"

"Well, I'm a writer, as I told you. My partner and I currently have the top-selling book of all time."

"Really?" I asked.

Right then my mind started clicking. If this guy was telling the truth, maybe I could get him to talk to some of his friends, and they could get me some of the materials I needed to help my homeless brothers and sisters survive the coming winter. I wondered what was the best way to approach him with the idea. The answer was simple. Jesus said, "Ask and you shall receive." So that's what I decided to do. Keep in mind that throughout this entire conversation I was heading toward the airport at 70 mph.

"Well, let me ask you a question, Mr. Hansen." I looked in the mirror and could tell by the look on his face that he thought I was going to hit him up for some money. But that wasn't my intention. Instead, I said, "I could sure use your help."

"Oh really, how?" he asked.

"Well, it's like this. If you speak all over the country and have a best-selling book, then you must have a lot of contacts and a lot of friends. I'm wondering if you might talk to them and see if they might send me materials to hand out this coming winter to help my brothers and sisters on the streets. You know, we need things like new and used clothing, long johns, hats, gloves, and basic things that will help keep people from dying on the streets this winter."

"Well, I guess I might be able to help you. When we get to the airport, give me your contact information. I'll need your name and phone number and the like, and I'll see what I can do. What was your name again?"

"Richard G. Tripp," I said.

"You know, Mr. Tripp, I'm thinking about putting a story about you in my next book. I'll let you know."

About that time, we pulled up to the airport, and I let him out. The porter got the bags out of the trunk, we said our good-byes, and Mark headed into the airport, but not before he gave me an autographed copy of *Chicken Soup for the Soul* as a tip. To this day, I don't think our meeting was an accident. I believe it was heavenly ordained. The feeling I'd had that morning had materialized in the form of an extraordinary person. Someone walked into my life that day, and that someone—Mr. Mark Victor Hansen, or "the teacher," as I often refer to him—has taught me how to help others in ways that I wouldn't have ever imagined could be possible.

Waiting Game

After our initial contact, I spent more than a month waiting for a letter or a phone call from Mr. Hansen. I started to think he may have told me what he had, just to stop me from bothering him. My plate was pretty full, and after a while I forgot about him. You can't actually forget an encounter like that, but you can put it in the back of your mind.

After all, it was October and I was busy preparing for my next Christmas morning event. Not only that, but I was still regaining my strength following that extended hospital stay. I was getting stronger and stronger each day, and I might add that I was also working longer and longer.

By that time, I had moved out of my daughter's house, and I had rented a little one-room apartment. It wasn't much, but it was mine as long as I could pay the rent. It was nice staying with my daughter, but to tell the truth, I couldn't stand some of her friends, and I felt like I was a burden on her. Let's face it, two members of the same family can't see eye to eye about everything.

I had been living in that one-room apartment for a couple of weeks when I got up one Saturday morning to go to work. As usual, I stopped at Quick-Trip to pick up some coffee and a newspaper before I headed for a hotel in search of a fare. I read the newspaper as I sat in line at a cabstand and waited for a fare. A glance at a photo in the newspaper's church guide caught my eye. The caption read, "Unity Church of Overland Park will host America's number one storyteller and the co-author of *Chicken Soup for the Soul,* Mark Victor Hansen, this Sunday at the morning service. He will also conduct a workshop Sunday afternoon from two until four." I couldn't believe it. Here he was, back in my area, and I hadn't heard from him.

I immediately decided that I would be in church Sunday morning. Going to church wasn't something I did very often. I was usually trying to get airport trips at the local hotels on Sunday mornings. But I wouldn't be doing that tomorrow. Tomorrow I was going to pay Mr. Hansen a special visit.

The next day, I pulled up to the address that the newspaper listed for the church. I parked my car and got up the courage to go inside. I had no idea what I was walking into. I was brought up a Southern Baptist. I had never been to a Unity church, so I really didn't know what to expect. You might say I was stepping out of my comfort zone, but Mark Victor Hansen was in that church, and I needed to find out why I hadn't heard from him. I still hadn't ruled out the possibility that he'd just fed me a line that day in my taxi.

I was greeted as soon as I walked into the church and asked my name. The greeter wrote it on a name tag and stuck it to my shirt. I proceeded to a pew in the back of the sanctuary and sat down. The service started. It was different from the services I had been to while growing up. For one thing, the minister was a woman. That sort of surprised me, but her sermon was excellent. Her name was Mary, and I was touched by her sermon. After listening to it, I gave her a nickname, "Angel Mary." The minister then announced that the morning's featured speaker was going to facilitate a workshop that afternoon. She introduced him, "Mr. Mark Victor Hansen," and out walked Mark.

Mark received a standing ovation as he walked out onto the platform. I had never witnessed anyone who carried that kind of a presence just by walking onto a stage. The people were going wild. I've seen it a lot since, but I'll never forget the first time. He was dressed just as nice as he had been the day I picked him up at the hotel, and he had to motion several times to get the people to sit down so he could speak. They were in awe of his presence. You would have thought the president or some high-ranking government official was on the platform.

Things quieted down, and he spoke. The speech he gave focused on a book he'd written about tithing, and how people should tithe. He also mentioned all the other books he had written, including *Chicken Soup for the Soul*, which at the time was the *New York Times* number-one seller.

As he finished speaking, he invited people to go out to the church lobby, where they could buy his books and have them autographed. I would guess that almost every person in that church bought at least one of his books. He had five or six titles on display in that lobby. There were books, tapes, DVDs, CDs, you name it. People were buying these things like crazy and getting in line to have them signed. They didn't seem to care that the line of people waiting for him to sign their books spanned the length of the church.

I stayed at the back of the line for at least an hour, waiting for him to finish signing all those books. When I finally got within speaking distance of him, he looked up from signing a book and saw me. The first thing out of his mouth was,

"Richard, I've been trying to get hold of you. I misplaced the address and phone number you gave me. I'm so glad you're here."

I was shocked. This guy, a man who I'm sure had met thousands of people since I'd given him a ride to the airport, remembered my name. It blew me away. Mark then started to introduce me to what was left of the crowd. He told them my story and mentioned that he was writing a story about me in his upcoming book. The people started shaking my hand and saying, "It's nice to meet you, Mr. Tripp."

The next thing Mark said to me was, "You're going come to my workshop this afternoon, aren't you?"

"Well, I hadn't planned on it," I said.

"Oh, you must come," he said.

I didn't tell him, but I couldn't afford to attend the workshop. However, I think he figured that out because he said, "You have to stay and be my guest this afternoon."

I said, "Well okay, Mark."

He was done signing books, so he said, "You come with me, Richard."

I followed him and Nancy Jerome, an associate pastor at the church, back to her office, where lunch was waiting for him. He asked me if I wanted anything, and I said, "A cup of coffee would be just fine."

Nancy, who has since become a very close friend, said, "I can handle that." With that, she left the room.

Mark and I sat there talking until it was time for him to start his workshop.

It seemed like most of the church had signed up to attend the workshop. I sat down and listened. About midway through the presentation, he started telling the audience about a friend of his who he was writing a story about in his new book. "Richard, would you come up here, please?"

People started clapping, and I was shocked. I wondered to myself, "Is he speaking to me?" I knew he was, but this was the last thing I'd expected when I'd gone to the church that morning. My legs felt like rubber, and my heart rate intensified as I headed toward the platform. He told the people about the work I'd been doing, and he shared the story I'd told him about the boy and his piggy bank. As Mark concluded the story, the crowd gave me a standing ovation.

I was standing on stage with Mark when he said, "Richard, why don't you say a few words." About the only thing I could think to say was that I was holding an event Christmas morning, and if anyone wanted to help they could give me a call. I handed the mic back to Mark and headed off the stage. The people must have liked what I'd said, because I got the same kind of standing ovation Mark had received when he'd taken the stage that morning.

After returning to my seat, several people approached me and asked for my card. I felt kind of stupid, because I didn't have one. I told them I would come back and drop some off later in the week. After that experience, I went out and had some printed. I wasn't going to get caught like that next time, and I had a feeling that there would be a next time.

After Mark finished his workshop, I took him to the airport. As I drove, we talked about the event I was planning for Christmas morning. He said he would be in touch, and he offered to write a letter to the church we'd just left to see if the congregation might be interested in helping me gather some winter clothing for the poor. He also volunteered to speak with some friends in the business world about my mission. He was hoping that they would help and spread the word. He didn't say who; he just said friends.

I had no idea how things were going to go. I just knew that things seemed to be looking up. I got him to the airport, and he told me he would be coming back to Kansas City in a week or two. He said he would give me a call to pick him up at the airport. I thanked him for his help, and he was gone.

Flat on My Face My Education in Homelessness Begins

It was a hot miserable August day in 1989; I was driving for one of the bigger taxi companies in town. I had long since been divorced from my wives and didn't see my kids very much. I had given up hope of ever getting my kids back from the Department of Social Services and foster care. I did, however, get to see Keith and Dawn once in awhile, and they let me see Ricky and Danny a couple times a month. I'd drive down to Nevada, Missouri to the welfare office and see the boys. But they didn't let me see my other girls, Jody or Christina. I was 44 years old and had become a working alcoholic and was staying in a kitchenette apartment usually when I wasn't drunk I was working. I didn't really have any plans for the future; I was just existing. I had just brought a fare down from the airport and was unloading him at one of the city's many hotels. The passenger was complaining because my cab lacked air conditioning. At that time, most of the taxis were not air conditioned. I had pulled a trick on the customer to get him into the car in the first place. As a lot of drivers did, I sat idling with all my windows rolled up. This made the potential fare think the cab was air conditioned. The practice wasn't good for tips, but at least I didn't miss out on the fare.

When I picked the fare up and got out on I-29, hi-way he immediately asked, "Where's the air?"

I said, "All you got to do is roll the window down."

The fare cussed from the time he got in the cab until we pulled up at the hotel. I got out, unlocked the trunk, and unloaded his oversized suitcase. As I did this, I felt a sharp pain in my lower back. When I straightened up, it felt like I had pulled something; I figured it was just a muscle. Needless to say, my passenger didn't give me a tip. I pulled off the hotel driveway and veered back into the taxi line. As I waited, I reached under the seat and pulled out the half pint of Canadian Mist I kept there. I drank it down quickly, figuring it would help the pain in my back, which it did. For the next few days, I continued to have a bit of pain every once in a while. Instead of going to see a doctor, I chose to self-medicate with the bottle. Not long after that, I got out of my taxi at the cab company and started across the parking lot, when suddenly my legs went numb. I fell flat on my face.

Some of the drivers who witnessed the accident laughed and joked around, saying, "Tripp tripped."

I got up, laughed it off, and said, "I guess I'll tie my shoelaces better next time." I knew something was wrong, but I didn't know what.

Over the course of the next few days, something else started happening. I'd be driving along and my legs would suddenly go numb as I pushed down on the brake or the gas. In one instance when my legs wouldn't operate, I almost had a wreck. Someone, probably another driver, had apparently seen me fall a couple of times and had snitched me out to the general manager of the taxi company.

The next day when I showed up to pick up my cab, the dispatcher stopped me. He said, "You have to see the boss before we can give you a car, Tripp."

"For what?" I inquired.

"I don't know, but they called down and said not to lease you a car until they talk to you."

"Okay, I'll go see what they want."

I went to the general manager's office and asked his secretary to let him know I was there.

She said, "Have a seat, Mr. Tripp. He'll be with you in a minute."

I sat there for about ten minutes before he came out of his office, motioned me in, and said, "Have a seat."

I sat down and asked, "What's the problem, Bill? How come dispatch said I had to see you before I could lease a car?"

"Well, Mr. Tripp, I've had several complaints from our customers. One of them said that one of our drivers almost had a wreck the other night while he was a passenger in one of our cabs."

"What's that got to do with me?"

"Well, Mr. Tripp, the cab number the customer gave was leased to you. This customer also gave a very detailed description of the driver. It fits you to a T. I've also heard from some of the drivers that they saw you fall flat on your face out there in the parking lot the other day."

"Bill, that was just because my shoestrings were untied."

"Well, that may be, Mr. Tripp, but it's like this, I can't let you lease another car until I get a doctor's statement confirming that you're fit to drive."

I jumped up and started cussing, "I haven't got the time or the money to go see a damn doctor."

"Well, I'm sorry then, because until you show me proof that a doctor has given you a clean bill of health, you won't be leasing any of our taxis."

"Well, screw you then. I'll go to another company," I yelled as I left his office.

I wasn't really mad at him for doing his job. I was really just scared at the prospects I'd be facing if I was unable to convince one of the other cab companies to lease me a cab. The next day I tried to go to another company, but word had gotten around that I had a problem, and nobody would lease me a car. My life suddenly spiraled out of control. For the first time, I didn't know what I was going do. I knew there wasn't any possible way I would pass a physical, so I didn't even bother to go see a doctor.

I had been renting a kitchenette apartment, but it only took one month of not being able to pay the rent to get me evicted. All I had left was my old Plymouth, so I started living in it. One good thing, if there was anything good about my situation, was that all those years I had driven a taxi; I had done a lot of camping. Therefore, I owned a lot of camping equipment. I had a butane single-burner stove, pots, pans, and so on. At least I was able to make myself a hot meal while I looked for work. And thank God I still had my old car. Not only was it serving as my sleeping quarters, but I could also take it down to the Greyhound Bus Station, where I would hang around and try to pick up money giving rides to people who couldn't afford to pay for a taxi. I hustled them at a cheaper price and made enough money to continue eating. The practice wasn't legal, and if I got caught I could go to jail for it. But this wasn't about breaking the law or not breaking the law; this was about survival.

Going Backward

One of the downsides to living in my car was that I didn't have any place to really take a shower or clean up. I did the best I could in the bathroom at the bus station, but naturally that wasn't as good as a bath. Another downside to living in the car was that I also had to sleep in the car. Because I was parked on the street in front of the bus station, I couldn't just lie down in the backseat. Doing that was risky. A man sleeping in the back of a car attracted too much attention from people walking by and from the police. Because of this, I most often slept sitting up in the driver's seat. The bus station was not on a good side of town. I had to keep vigilant of what transpired around my vicinity so that I didn't get robbed or ripped off. I had that little one-burner propane stove in my trunk. At night when there wasn't anyone around, I would often cook a hot dog or an egg. I could even warm up a can of soup or chili without drawing too much attention. It wasn't an ideal living experience, but it was survival.

After a few weeks of being homeless, the old Plymouth quit on me. The transmission was slipping so badly that the only way I could get it to move was to drive it in reverse. I was at the Greyhound Bus Station when it finally refused to go forward anymore. Because I didn't have the money to fix it, I decided to junk it. That decision put me on foot, but I didn't have a choice at the time. I could either try to get the car to the junkyard and make a few dollars, or I could let the city tow it. If the city towed the car, I wouldn't make anything off it.

Before the car gave out on me, I had been able to earn enough money hauling people around to buy the simple foods I needed. That Plymouth had basically been my home and my lifeline. I didn't really know what I was going to do when I sold it, but at the time I didn't have a choice.

The question I faced at that moment was, "How am I going to get the car to the junkyard?" If I had the junkyard pick it up, I wouldn't get as much money for it as I would if I drove the car in. So I decided that I was going to drive the car to the junkyard. How, you ask? Why, in reverse over Truman Road, of course.

I knew driving my car backward for more than ten miles was going to be the ultimate test of my driving abilities. I also knew that I would have to accomplish this feat at a time when there wasn't much traffic on the road. I waited until about one o'clock one early morning before I attempted to make the trip. I had planned out my route to miss most of the traffic that would be traveling the road at that time of the morning. Of course, one obstacle I hoped not to face was running into the police and having to explain what I was doing. I figured that if I took my time and picked the right route, I just might make it to the junkyard without any problems. I started by backing up Troost to Eleventh Street. Backing around onto Eleventh Street was the hardest part. Once I got the car straightened out, it was a lot easier. You see, Eleventh Street was a one-way going west across Kansas City. All I had to do was get on it and watch for cars moving toward me as I headed east backward on Eleventh Street. The ten-mile drive wasn't easy, but I guess luck was with me, because I didn't see a single a police officer during my drive that night. I did run into some difficulty making a backward turn off Eleventh Street heading toward Fifteenth Street, where the junkyard was located. It took me until about four o'clock in the morning to get to the junkyard. I then had to wait for them to open at eight. I decided to lie back and got some sleep. The junkyard owner woke me in the morning and gave me one hundred dollars for the car. It hurt having to let that car go for one hundred dollars when just a few months earlier I had spent close to one thousand dollars having the engine rebuilt, but I didn't have a choice at that point. I took the cash and got my belongings out of the car.

The junkyard was about a mile from the side of town where I'd spent my childhood. I knew there were some woods up that way. I had played in them a lot as a child. I collected my belongings and headed for those woods to think. I needed to figure out what I should do next. I thought I might camp out up there since the surroundings were familiar; I knew those woods like the back of my hand. I had built camps up there as a kid. We'd played, built forts, had weenie roasts; we'd done all the normal things kids do out in the woods. However, as a child I never dreamed that I would end up living in those woods for a few months as an adult. It was summer, and I figured I could hold up out there until I could get something going or find a place to live.

Those woods stretched from Truman Road on the south side to Independence Avenue on the north side, and they stretched from I-435 on the west side to Blue Ridge on the east side. Altogether the woods covered about one square mile of ground right in the middle of the east side of Kansas City. I might add that there were all kinds of wildlife in those woods. There was everything from snakes to deer and even wild turkey. I decided to make a camp right in the middle of those woods. The hardest part would be getting drinking water. I would have to carry it in jugs from the gas station on Truman Road.

One positive aspect of the location I'd chosen to make my camp was that the whole area was loaded with caves where there had once been a rock quarry. There were miles of limestone caves with lots of entrances. They were made when workers ground up rock for gravel. Once they'd removed the rock, parts of the caves were used for storage. Being inside one felt like having air conditioning, and there were plenty of them out there with nothing stored in them. When it really got hot during the day, a person could cool off in those caves.

But all good things come to an end, and it wasn't long before I was out of money and supplies. In our community, like other communities across America, there were churches that had food banks in them. I started frequenting these various food banks for the canned goods and other foodstuffs they handed out. I usually found out which churches handed out food by talking to other homeless people at the different soup kitchens. The only time I had a problem was on days when the food bank handed out meat. I would have to cook it the same day I got it, because it was hard to keep it from spoiling without refrigeration. The only refrigeration I had at the campsite was an ice chest, but most of the time I couldn't afford the ice to put in it. At most of the churches, all you had to do to get groceries was show them some type of ID.

The only money I had coming in came from working out of the day-labor pools. I would have to get up at about three in the morning and hitchhike downtown to be at the labor pool by six when it opened. I had a wind up-alarm clock that I set each night to make sure I was up that early. The problem with hitchhiking was that you never knew if you were going to be able to get a ride, and you never knew who you were getting in the car with. Only once did I have a problem after being picked up hitchhiking. The guy who picked me up got into a fender bender while I was in the car. No one was hurt, so I just got out of his car and started hitchhiking from the scene of the accident like nothing had happened. The problem with the labor pools was that if you didn't make it to their place by six o'clock, your odds of landing a job for the day weren't good. There were many times I didn't make it in time because I was unable to get a ride. Another problem with the labor pools was you never knew when you would be put out on a job, and you never knew what type of job you would be given. You really had no choice in the matter. You were to consider yourself lucky that you had an opportunity to work at all. You could sit there all week from six in the morning until six at night and not get put on a job. Of course, there were both good jobs and bad jobs. A good job might be washing dishes at a restaurant, while one of the bad jobs might be unloading one-hundred-pound sacks of potatoes off a boxcar. Of course, the most coveted jobs were the good jobs that came with return tickets. Having a return ticket meant you might work at the same place for a couple of weeks, but those jobs were few and far between. If you were lucky enough to get a return-ticket job, you tried your damnedest to hold onto it. You were there every morning at six o'clock, because if you weren't, they would give the ticket to another worker. During that time, I lost several good jobs because of tardiness. If I was lucky enough to get a job, I would almost always take a city bus back to my campsite at the end of the day. If I didn't get a job, I would hitchhike home, just like I'd hitchhiked to the labor pool that morning.

I started asking other homeless and poor people what they did in the winter. I needed to know how they survived. A lot of them said they went to shelters, but a lot of them said they didn't. They told me stories about the different shelters. I heard about the good ones and the bad ones, and I heard a lot of horror stories about the way some people were treated at the shelters. But I didn't have much choice; I had to do something. When it started getting cold outside, I decided to give the shelter system a try, at least for the winter.

The Homeless Shelter—One Man's Hope, Another Man's Hell

The front entrance of the shelter looked nice enough when I showed up that fall day in 1989. The problem is that looks can be deceiving. I tried to enter through the front door and was stopped by a staff member, who asked what I needed. I told him why I was there, and he told me that transients had to use the backdoor. I was to go around to the backside of the building in order to gain entry.

I went around to the backside of the building and found the entrance marked "Transients." I quickly learned that the back entrance was a lot different than the front of the building. It consisted of a gate that led into a little yard-type setting, with a sidewalk that went to a door on the back of the building. The fence that was attached to the gate was about twelve feet tall, with razor wire hanging over the top of it. As a matter of fact, that entrance looked more like a prison yard than a shelter. I saw about twenty guys standing in that little enclosure, smoking, drinking coffee, and visiting. I continued inside the back door and was asked by another staff member if I wanted a bed for a night.

I said, "Yes."

He said, "Well, go in the day room. They start lining up for beds at five. You'll have to get in line."

"Where is the day room?" I asked.

"Go through that door and turn right," he said.

I did what he said and found myself in the day room for the very first time. It was a strange experience for me. It was a room that must have measured about fifty feet long by twenty feet wide. There were old chairs and men scattered about the room. In the southwest corner of the room there was a desk, and sitting behind that desk was a staff member who was taking down names and assigning beds. The place smelled terrible. Some of the men in the room looked like they never changed their clothes. Others were sick, and you could tell that some of the guys had either been drinking or were coming off a drunk. There was a mixture of disgusting traits in that room. You name it, and it was represented in that room. Men from age sixteen to ninety were present. There were guys yelling, cussing, and talking to themselves. There must have been a couple of hundred guys in that room. I hadn't really expected this kind of indoctrination to the shelter system, but I was already there, so I just sat down in one of the chairs and waited for the five o'clock lineup for bed call. At about quarter to five, one of the staff members yelled, "Everybody line up for bed call."

Everybody jumped up and got in line to get a tag for their bed. It was crazy. I guessed that people were trying to jump in line ahead of others so they could get a better bed. But I soon found out that one was as good as the other. Still, every night people tried to jump in front of others. It was a hassle, and it wasn't just for beds. It seemed like this happened for everything.

If there was a line forming, then there was always someone trying to jump it. This often led to fights. Sometimes it really got out of hand. I mean, you could get hurt bad by jumping the line for an old, stale sandwich. That may sound like an immature statement, but I can assure you, I have seen it happen numerous times. It happened at bedtime; it happened at chow time; it happened when donated clothes were being passed out; it happened just about any time something was being given away for free.

After the bed tags were handed out, the shelter staff would have everybody line up for chapel service. At this particular shelter, the chapel services were held on the second floor. If you were going to spend that night, you had to go to chapel service and listen to a sermon before you were led into the kitchen to get something to eat. The shelter staff led the group up a set of stairs that led to the chapel and the kitchen. Most of the transients didn't like that they had to listen to a sermon before they ate. At the same time, they knew it wouldn't do any good to complain. If you wanted to eat the shelter's food, you had to go by the shelter's rules.

After listening to an hour of preaching, the men were led into the kitchen for supper. The meal usually consisted of a two-or three-day-old sandwich off a catering truck. Half the time, the meat was greenish looking because it had been warmed so many times. But to the shelter operators, these men were just transients. Actually, they weren't even transients. In my opinion, each one represented a number that needed to be counted to keep the money coming in for the shelter's programs. Of course, better treatment was available. All it required was that a transient sign up for the shelter's so-called Christian Life Program and become a member of their staff. As a member of the Christian Life Program there was good food to eat, the best clothes to wear, and just about anything else you wanted. Of course, those who signed up had to live at the shelter for sixty days while attending classes, and there were a lot of rules to follow. But if you opted for the Christian Life Program, the shelter life could be good to you.

I'm sorry. I just wasn't cut out for that kind of lifestyle. It felt too much like a cult. Besides, I never did think Jesus would make hungry men listen to a story about him before he gave them something to eat.

After eating supper, the men were led into a hallway, where the shelter staff took their clothes in exchange for something that resembled a nightgown. The men were told to take a shower, put on their nightgown, and prepare for bed in one of the dorms.

One of the bad things about the way they ran the shelter was that when you gave them your clothes, they would put them in a locker basket and give you a key to the basket. Many times, you'd get your clothes and possessions back the next day, and things would be missing, stolen by someone on the staff. Also, if you made a staff member mad for any little reason, he or she could have you barred from the shelter. The staff members acted like they were better than the transients because they were staff members of the shelter. The majority of the staff members at one time had been homeless themselves. And everyone knows that oftentimes when you give a little bit of power to a person who's never had any authority, they let it go to their heads.

This shelter, like many others, also played games with the donating public. The challenge is to keep the donations coming in no matter what. The game is to make the public believe that donated materials are being used in the way the donor intended. For instance, when you give clothing to a shelter, most of the items never make it into the hands of the people in need; at least the good stuff doesn't. If some staff member doesn't grab it, then it goes to the shelter's thrift store to be sold. In my opinion, this is a practice that the majority of the shelters follow.

One of the cons this particular shelter ran was that they would get people to donate coffee, sugar, and cream to the shelter so they could in turn give it to their homeless clients. The problem was that they were getting it for free but charging their clients money for each cup of coffee. In the same regard, when good food was donated, it never made it into the transients' stomachs. However, it always seemed to find its way to the staff members. I'd like to say these cons were only happening at that one shelter, but that would be a lie. I know it happens all over the country. I have heard the same stories from homeless brothers and sisters staying in shelters around the country. These are minor problems to the homeless, but they are just the tip of the iceberg of the atrocities being committed on those down and out.

Believe me when I tell you that there is so much going on behind the scenes at different shelters across America—not just in my city. For one, most have staffing problems. Most of the staff is untrained, and many shelters do not run background checks on their staff members.

For instance, I was told about a shelter that had a chaplain on its payroll for years. He was stationed at one of the men's shelters, and he was married to a real nice lady who happened to be the chaplain at one of the women's shelters nearby. They were hiding behind the guise of being clergy and most of the town held this couple in high regard. In reality, they were perverts who used poor and homeless men and women to fulfill their sexual desires. I don't think I have to spell it out for you. It's hard to keep a story like that hidden, and eventually the stories came out. I was told about it by some of the homeless brothers and sisters that had said they had been victimized by this couple. It seems the couple left the shelters they had used as their own personal sexual playgrounds before anyone had a chance to do anything about it. I don't know where they ended up, but you see you here of incidents like that happening in shelters across America all the time.

Gangs present another real, life-threatening problem within the shelters. You get a group of guys hanging out at a shelter, and the shelter operator's end up using them to do their bidding, so to speak. Let's say you complain to someone about an injustice that occurred at the shelter, and the story got in the news. The operators of that shelter might use their little gang of regulars to get you to leave town, physically harm you, or at least scare you into being quiet and not returning to that shelter. And as long as the threats are made away from the shelter, no one is ever the wiser. For this, the gang members might receive extra comforts.

I am now aware of these things, and I know what to look for, but back then I had no idea of the games being played on my homeless brothers and sisters. From the day I walked into my first shelter, I began to learn the system. I also vowed to make it my personal goal to make a difference in the way these people were being treated.

You might be asking yourself the same question I asked myself when I saw through all the injustices that were being committed against the poor. "What would Jesus do?" I didn't know the answer, but after thinking about the question, I knew I had to at least try to make a difference. What I did know was that if Jesus Christ had been there, he would have done something.

Enough Is Enough

After staying at that shelter nightly for a few months, I had finally seen enough hurt and injustice brought upon different brothers in the name of Jesus. I knew that if I was the Christian I believed myself to be, then I had to try to make some changes in the way these men were being treated. The question was, "How?"

One morning, after being put out of the shelter at six o'clock, I went around to the front and waited across the street for the shelter's director to show up. The director never visited the day room where people would sign up for beds, but he occasionally delivered the mandatory sermons the transients attended before being given a meal. It must have been seven thirty or so when I saw him park his car in the parking lot across the street from the shelter.

I waited for him to start to walk across the street. Then I walked up to him and said, "Sir, I would like to speak to you about the way the transients are being treated."

"What's your name, Son?" he inquired.

"Richard Tripp, sir."

"Well, Mr. Tripp, if you want to speak to me about something, visit my secretary today. She'll set up an appointment so we can talk. Right now, I've got to run. I'm late for an appointment."

With that he continued across the street and into the building. I sort of felt like I had done the right thing by catching him when he arrived at work, even if he didn't have time to speak to me. He was a short, stocky, white gentleman. I guess he must have been in his sixties, and he wore wire-brimmed glasses. He was dressed casually in a blue blazer, and he had seemed like a nice enough guy when I approached him. I actually had heard him preach a couple times. He was your typical hell-and-brimstone Baptist preacher when he gave a sermon, but when I spoke to him that morning, he'd come off sort of laid back. Later that day, I set up an appointment to speak with him later that week.

The day of the appointment, he invited me into his office and said, "Have a seat. I'm sorry, what was your name again?"

"Richard Tripp, sir."

"Okay, Mr. Tripp. You said something about complaints the other day when I saw you?"

"Yes, sir, I did."

"Well, what sort of complaints do you have?"

We sat there for about twenty minutes. I explained some of the injustices I had seen while staying there, and I explained how some of his staff members were treating the transients at the shelter.

He seemed to be genuinely interested in my concerns. He finally said, "Well, Mr. Tripp, I'll look into your concerns."

He thanked me and opened his door so I could go back down to the day room. When I left his office and headed down the stairs, I felt like I had really made a difference. I had felt at ease speaking to him, probably because I had been brought up in the Baptist faith, and I was happy that he'd been receptive to my complaints.

Up until that meeting, I had seen a lot of injustices done to others, but I really hadn't had any problems of my own. However, after that meeting, things started turning bad for me personally. The staff members, ones who had seemed to like me at one time, started making wisecracks like, "There's the man that don't like the way things are done here. Maybe he had better find somewhere else to stay before he gets hurt." Things like money, food, and stamps started coming up missing from my personal belongings. When I complained to the staff, I was told, "If you think something is missing, then maybe you should find another place to stay."

These problems continued for a few weeks, and I just let them ramble on. Then something happened that messed with my spirit. Two separate incidents occurred to two different homeless brothers that left me with no other choice but to take a stand.

One incident involved a nineteen-year-old kid who had shown up at the shelter from out of town. He left his bag with one of the staff members in the holding room, a room where the transients were encouraged to leave their bags while attending chapel and dinner. While the boy was at dinner, a staff member either misplaced or threw the bag out. At any rate, the kid was told that if he didn't like it, he could leave.

The kid started crying, "But my grandpa's pictures are in that bag. He just died, and those are my only copies."

It was then that one of the black staff members told the boy, "Well, man, you seen one old white man, you seen them all."

I lost it. I grabbed that staff member, pinned him against a door, and said, "You find that kid's bag."

"Hey, man, let me go," the staff member replied.

I let him go just about the time a couple of other staff members showed up wanting to know what was going on.

I said, "This kid needs his bag."

The staff member that I had pinned against the door told the other staff members, "That guy Tripp grabbed me and threw me up against the door."

They looked at me, and one of them said, "You can't be grabbing staff members."

I said, "But …" and tried to explain what had happened. But the senior staff member said, "I don't care what was said or what happened here. You're barred for a week. Get your stuff and get out."

I knew I had blown it, so I grabbed my bag and left. To this day I don't know what happened to that kid, but in my mind I can still see him standing there crying. Let me clarify that if a white staff member had made that comment to a black kid, I would have had the same reaction.

The second incident that persuaded me to take a stand for my homeless brothers and sisters happened as I returned to the shelter after having lunch at one of the downtown Kansas City food kitchens. As I rounded the corner to go into the shelter, I heard a commotion on the backside of the building, just outside the fence. There were five guys beating up on one little guy.

Without thinking, I started to run across the street to help. But before I could reach the mob, one of the attackers pulled out a knife and stabbed the victim several times. When the attackers saw me coming, they took off running. I ran up to the man who had been stabbed and tried to help him. I took off my coat and put it around him to try to keep him warm. That was really about all I could do, aside from yelling to the people in the shelter and telling them to call 911.

Both an ambulance and the police arrived shortly thereafter, and the man was taken to the hospital. The police asked me a lot of questions, but there wasn't really much I could tell them. It had all happened so fast. Later that day I wanted to know how the man was doing, so I headed over to Truman Medical Center to check on him. I found out the guy was in X-ray, and I convinced the nurses to let me go up and see how he was doing.

When I got up to where he was being X-rayed, I heard a bone-chilling yell followed by, "Oh God, that hurts!" It was him. The victim was talking to a doctor who was trying to stitch up one of the stab wounds. The victim had four or five different stab wounds, and the nurse told me they would be admitting him if he survived. I entered the room long enough to let him know someone cared, to make sure he knew he wasn't alone, and to tell him that I'd be back to check on him. I then left and walked back to the shelter.

Later that day, I learned why the man had been attacked. One of the five attackers had jumped in line in front of the man during the lunch rush. As a result of their squabble, both men had been thrown out of the shelter. The line jumper decided that he and some of his friends were going to beat up this little guy. I don't believe they intended to kill him, but I believe he was holding his own in the fight, and that's why the knife came into play. For a spot in a line to get a sandwich, a man had almost lost his life that day.

Months later, I became friends with the man who had been attacked, and I tried to get him off the streets. As a matter of fact, I found him a job as a janitor at an apartment building. But the streets beat me to him. I had a job and a home lined up for him, and I put the word out that anyone who knew where he was should tell him to get in touch with me, pronto. A few days later, I was told by a police officer that the man had been found beaten to death in a park not far from the shelter. If I had been able to get to him just a few days sooner, maybe I could have changed the way things turned out. I have no idea if it was the same men that had attacked him at the shelter that were the ones that killed him or not, but it could have been.

After running those guys off that had attacked that gentleman, I figured I had better steer clear of that shelter for awhile to avoid another confrontation with those guys. I decided to try another shelter across town.

Reporting the Truth

There was a little shelter down by the city market on Fifth Street. It was little compared to the other shelters in the city, but I thought it might be a good place to stay, because it was near the market and every once in a while you could get a job cleaning things up around the market. Also, plenty of produce and the like got thrown away down at the market. If you were really hungry, you could go through the Dumpsters to get something to eat.

I had been staying there for a few weeks when one day I was standing in line across the street from the shelter, waiting for it to open up. I guess there were about twenty of us waiting when up walked a couple of female reporters. They said they were doing a story about homelessness in the city for one of the area's newspapers. Most of the guys just avoided them. They didn't want to make any comments. One of the reporters was named CJ. She walked over, introduced herself to me, and asked me what I thought of the shelters in Kansas City.

"Not much," I replied.

That was the opening she needed for her story. Among a lot of other questions, she asked me how I had ended up homeless. I felt at ease talking to her, but I didn't realize at the time that I was talking myself into what would become one of the biggest scandals to hit the city in a long time. The stories I told her would eventually make me one of the most talked about people among the not-for-profits in my city. I also didn't realize that my stories would make Richard G. Tripp a name that some of those not-for-profits would worry about every time it was mentioned.

Of course, all that would come later. For the present, I let her know some of the scams that were going on. I told her so much that I think she had a problem believing everything I was telling her.

At the end of the interview she asked, "Mr. Tripp, can you prove any of the things you have told me?"

I looked at her and said, "Listen, everything I've told you is pretty much common knowledge among the homeless. I can't really prove these things, but I can put you in touch with some of the homeless people that the different injustices have happened to and also some of the staff members of that one shelter. They know the truth. I can let you know who they are, but I can't make them talk to you, CJ."

"Okay, just let me know who they are. I'll take it from there," she said.

"Okay," I replied. I gave her a list of names and told her where she might find some of the people hanging out.

She thanked me and said she would look me up if she needed any more information. She then asked where she could find me.

I said, "I'm not hard to find. Just come to this shelter."

After she and her friend left, a couple of the homeless brothers came over and started talking to me.

"What did you tell her?" one of them asked.

"The truth," I replied.

"You didn't really, did you?" the same guy asked.

I shook my head and said, "Yes, I did. Why?"

"Oh man, you're in some deep shit now," another said.

"What do you mean?" I asked.

"Don't you know that if they print stuff and use your name and the shelters find out you had something to do with it, they'll blackball you? You won't be able to stay at a shelter. They might even get mad enough to take you out?" he said.

"You've got to be kidding," I said.

"Hell no, I'm not kidding. I'm sure glad I'm not in your shoes, my friend."

I started to think that maybe I'd gone too far by talking to that reporter. Others in the line heard my brothers and me talking, and they chimed in with their opinions. Some of them said I did the right thing. Others were convinced that I'd messed up. At any rate, it was too late to do anything about it. The reporters were gone, and I had lit the ember that would start the fire.

A few weeks had gone by with no repercussions. I was standing in line at that same shelter when up walked CJ.

She said, "Mr. Tripp, I just stopped by to let you know that I did do the story on the homeless that you helped me with. It will be in our paper this Thursday, so be looking for it."

"Did the people I put you in contact with talk to you?" I asked.

"Yes, they did. We also got some people on the inside to fill us in on a lot. Oh, by the way, I just thought I'd tell you that I believe everything you told me a few weeks ago. And I also believe the homeless of our city will thank you for getting involved."

With those words she left, but I was really starting to get worried. How much had she printed about what I had told her? And worse yet, had she mentioned my name? I would have to wait until Thursday to find out.

Shelter Skelter

On Thursday morning, I was awoken at five o'clock, just like every morning at the Fifth Street shelter. I took a fast shower and ate what they considered breakfast—a cup of coffee and a bowl of oats. There was no sugar, no milk, just oats. The transients at that shelter were expected to shower, eat, and be ready to walk out the door by five-thirty in the morning. That was the normal routine.

That particular morning, a couple of guys I had befriended decided to go with me to McDonald's for coffee. At five in the morning, there isn't much open downtown except the City Center Square McDonald's at Twelfth and Main. It's about a mile from the shelter. Most of the transients head there early in the morning. If they're lucky enough to have money for a cup of coffee, they will sit at McDonald's until things such as the labor pools or the library start opening up. If they don't have money, they'll often loiter around the property until someone throws away their cup. Then one of the transients will retrieve the cup from the trash and get a refill, as if they'd bought the cup of coffee in the first place. They do this to avoid being hassled by security. You won't get messed with if you look like you've made a purchase.

On that particular morning, I happened to have enough money to buy a cup of coffee for myself and one for each of the guys accompanying me. The money was change from some food stamps I'd used the day before.

I had known these guys for several weeks now. One of them was an older guy nicknamed "Abe." The other guy was about 43, my age at the time. His nickname was "Pockets." For the most part, people on the streets don't use their real names. Most of them go by nicknames. Don't ask me how they get their names. It just happens that way with people on the street.

Anyway, we were sitting there drinking our coffee when Abe says, "Hey, Tripp, isn't that article supposed to be in the paper today?"

"That's what that reporter said," I replied.

Pockets interrupted and said, "Well, I'll have to get a paper and see what they wrote."

"It probably won't be much," I said.

"I hope it is," he replied. "Somebody has to do something about the way people are being treated up there on Troost Street."

I nodded my head and said, "Well, we'll have to wait until about noon, when they start dropping those papers off."

Abe changed the subject, "I wonder what they're going have for lunch at the church today."

"Who knows," I said. "You know their new cook has really been doing a good job since he's been there."

The church we were talking about was at Thirteenth and Broadway. They fed the poor and homeless every weekday between the hours of noon and two. It was the best meal the poor could get downtown. It was also a gathering place where the homeless could sit and talk to their friends or make new friends. There were other hangouts, but that church was the place you went to hear about everything that was going on in the city. You could find out if there were new shelters opening; you could get information about where you might acquire free clothing; or you might find out which pharmacies would fill prescriptions for free. The church was a homeless hub.

Abe, Pockets, and I sat at McDonald's until about six thirty. That's when we decided to go check out the labor pools to see if we could get a job for the day. We all agreed that if we didn't get on at one of the labor pools, we would meet at the church at lunchtime. There are several different day-labor pools people can go to in search of a job, so we went our separate ways.

My luck getting a job that day wasn't good. At about eleven thirty, I started walking toward the church. It was only about a fifteen-minute walk from the particular labor pool where I'd been. It had been my plan to stop at a paper box on the way to the church, but the first one I came to hadn't been changed to the new paper yet, so I continued westbound on Twelfth Street to the intersection of Twelfth and Wyandotte.

The paper stand there had been changed, so I pulled one of the papers out of the box. I looked at the front page and didn't see anything about the homeless. I opened the paper and started checking each page. I was about halfway through the paper when I turned a page and was shocked by what I saw. In giant letters, the headline on the page screamed, SHELTER SKELTER. Below the headline was a picture of the shelter and the gentleman who was the head of it. I started reading the article. It wasn't long before I came to my name. I was cited as one of the people who had helped break the story—myself and ex-staff members from the shelter.

The gentleman who ran the shelter had a smile on his face in the picture, but I don't think he had a smile on his face after reading the article. For some reason, he admitted to a lot of the things I had told CJ. I really couldn't believe the whole thing. He had in essence told on himself.

I continued to the church to get something to eat. When I got there, my buddies, Pockets and Abe, were already there. They saw me headed across the parking lot and ran over to me.

"Tripp, you did it."

"Did what?" I asked.

"You did them good," Pockets said.

"What you mean?" I asked.

"Didn't you read the paper?" Pockets asked.

"Yes, but I don't really think the article was that good."

"Are you nuts, Tripp? Everybody is talking about how you stood up to them and how you brought everything out to the public."

I didn't tell Pockets or Abe, but while I was glad the story was out, I was sorry it had come out the way it had. If that minister would have just made a few changes, I wouldn't have spoken to the reporters. I was also scared, because the shelter definitely knew who had helped with the story. Quotes from "the homeless man, Tripp," were all over the story. I wondered not only what repercussions I would have to face, but when I would have to face them.

Retribution

For the first seven to ten days after the story came out in the paper, I was treated like some kind of saint by my poor and homeless brothers and sisters. But after a while, a tension developed in the air. I think everyone knew that sooner or later something bad was going to happen to me. They just didn't know where and when it would happen. After a while, some people were afraid to be seen with me; they didn't want to be connected to me. I really think they were scared, and to tell you the truth, I was a little scared too. There were so many different rumors going around. I'd heard that the shelter was going to run me out of town. I also heard that they were going to have a bunch of guys beat me up. There was even a rumor that I had cost them so much they were going to hire a hit man to take care of me.

One thing I hadn't thought about when I decided to talk to those reporters is just how much all the different shelters and homeless organizations stick together. In other words, if you take on one, the rest back them up. It doesn't really matter if you're right or wrong. They cover for each other. I found that out the hard way.

It happened like this. About ten days after the article had appeared in the newspaper, I went to the shelter on Fifth Street in search of a bed for the night. I was sitting at the table waiting for a bowl of beans when one of their staff members came in and said, "Tripp, the director would like to speak to you. Go upstairs to his office."

I went up to his office and knocked on the door.

"Come in," he said.

I walked in and he said, "Have a seat."

I sat there looking at him. I really couldn't figure out what he wanted. I finally said, "What's up, Joe?"

He said, "Mr. Tripp, it's been reported to me that you were seen last night smoking downstairs, and we can't have it. You'll have to leave."

"You've got to be kidding," I said.

"Nope. Those are our rules," he replied.

"But you know it's after seven. No other shelter will let me in tonight."

He looked at me and said, "Well, my hands are tied."

Right then I knew I was being set up. I also knew it would do no good to tell Joe that I didn't even have enough money for a cigarette last night. Nothing I said would have mattered. You see, the other shelters, the good-old-boys network as I like to call them, had put on the pressure to get me to leave town. I'm very sure of that. Joe was simply their tool of execution. I don't think he liked doing it, but the politics and pressure from the others was too great.

So, at about seven thirty that crisp November night, I was put out on the street and told not to return for at least two weeks. It was ten to fifteen degrees outside, and it was raining ice. I remember looking up at the sky and saying, "Hey, God, what am I going to do? I did what I thought you wanted me to do, so now what? I mean, I'll probably die out here tonight. I know I can't get into another shelter, and it's so cold I'll likely freeze. But Lord, just in case I don't die and you see me through this, I promise that not one of those shelters will forget this night."

You might say it was then that I knew what direction my life was going to take if I lived through that night. I was going to do everything in my power to make sure the shelter system never pulled this on another human being. At the same time, I was going to make a difference for everyone who was being mistreated by the systems that plagued my community.

It was a really cold night. The weather was downright terrible. There weren't very many cars on the street, and it was raining ice, so the streets were slick. I barely made it up the hill from the shelter. I didn't really have any idea where I could go to get in out of the storm. Then it hit me. There was one place downtown that I knew would be open. I immediately headed for the police station at Twelfth and Locust. It took me at least an hour, maybe more, to get there. It seemed that for every step I took forward, I slid two back on the pavement. By the time I got to my destination, I was almost frozen. I think that may have been the only time in my life I was glad there was a police station open. I sat in that lobby the entire night.

When I left the next morning, I headed for the Homeless Information Center at Ninth and McGee. They opened at six o'clock, and they had a day center where you could sit and stay out of the cold. They closed between eleven and one for lunch. During those hours, most people walked over to the church on Thirteenth and Broadway to get something to eat. That's what I did. When I got to the church, Abe and Pockets were there.

They sat at my table, and Abe said, "Sorry to hear what happened to you last night."

"That's okay. I survived," I replied.

"Where did you go?" he asked.

"The only place I could think to go was the police station," I told him.

"How long did the shelter say you were barred?"

"They said a couple weeks."

"Well, what are you going to do tonight?"

"Abe, I don't really know. Maybe I'll go back to the police station. You know that the word is out. No matter what shelter I go to, they'll come up with some reason not to let me in."

Abe shook his head in agreement.

About that time, Pockets spoke up. He said, "Hey, Tripp, have you got any blankets hid anywhere?"

"Nope," I replied.

"Well, I have some hid down by the market. You're welcome to them if you need them."

"Thanks," I said, "But as cold as it is, I don't think they'll do me a lot of good out in the open."

He smiled, "I didn't say anything about out in the open, did I?"

"Okay, Pockets, what you got on your mind?" I asked.

"Well, down there by the railroad tracks, just north of the market, there's a broke down truck trailer that's been there for a couple months. Back during the summer I stayed in it for a couple months, and nobody ever bothered me. Maybe you could use it until you find somewhere to stay. All you would need to do is get some of the plastic the truckers use to wrap their loads down at the market. You could make a pretty snug place in that trailer to sleep at night."

"How many blankets you got, Pockets?" I inquired.

"I don't know for sure, three or four."

"Would that be enough to keep me warm in this weather?" I asked.

"Like I said, Tripp, if you get some of that plastic wrap at the market, it'll keep you warm."

"Okay, Pockets. After lunch show me where the trailer and blankets are. It looks like I'm going to be camping out tonight."

With the conversation over, we ate our lunches and then set out for the trailer. On the way, we stopped and picked up the blankets Pockets had hidden under a bunch of brush down by the tracks. They were in one of those old green trash bags. Anyone seeing them would have thought someone had just thrown out some trash. We continued on to the truck trailer.

To tell the truth, when I saw it, I had my doubts about staying there. The opening where the doors were was full of trash about five feet high. I said, "Pockets, it's full of trash."

"Tripp, just crawl over the trash. There's a good-size space on the other side of the trash."

I did what he told me to do, and sure enough, about ten feet into the trailer there was a space about twenty feet long. It was big enough to camp in. The best part was that people outside of the trailer couldn't tell anyone was inside, and only Pockets, Abe, and I knew I was staying there. I decided that it would be a safe hangout until the heat from the shelters died down. If somehow the word got out that I was down there, I doubted anyone would bother to crawl over the trash to find me.

It was sometime between two and three o'clock when Abe and Pockets took off.

I headed off to the market area to find some plastic so I could construct my little shelter. At least I had a place to plan whatever it was I was going do. As bad as I hate to say it, payback was very much on my mind. Aside from wanting revenge for what I'd personally gone through, I wanted to show them—the shelters and other organizations—that they couldn't treat people as less than human and get away with it.

Dog, St. Louis, and Two Feathers

That trailer turned out to be a good place to stay at night. I'd leave for most of the day and go back after dark, when no one would see me going in or out. It was the winter of 1990, and it was a cold one. But I had a warm spot in the back of that trailer. Still, I'd have preferred having a place where I could get undressed and take a shower.

I had traded some food stamps for another little one-burner stove that used the little butane tanks. The one I had stopped working so I had to get another. If it got real cold, I could warm up my spot with it and do light cooking at the same time. I had some candles too. They provided me with light at night so I could read. If I do say so myself, it wasn't a bad camp I'd set up inside that trailer.

A couple of old stray dogs I found down by the river followed me back to the trailer one night. One was male and looked like a German shepherd mix; the other was female, and I think she was a collie mix. The German shepherd was the bigger of the two. I gave him the name Bones, because he was nothing more than a big bag of bones when I first found him. However, by the time I gave him away to another homeless guy, Bones had probably gained thirty pounds. I'd named the collie mix Tag. This was because anytime I left the trailer without tying her up, she would try to tag along. I ended up giving both dogs to homeless guys living down on the river. I hated giving them away, but I knew I wouldn't have any place to keep them when I moved into the new shelter that had opened up.

I had kept up my daily routine of going to the labor pools, eating at the church, and visiting with friends like Pockets and Abe. One day while I was at the church eating lunch, I heard there was a new shelter opening up. I figured I would check it out. Seeing how it was new, I figured they might not know about me and the trouble I'd had with the other shelters.

I waited for nighttime to fall before I went and checked them out. This shelter was a lot different. As a matter of fact, you really couldn't call it a shelter. To begin with, it was in the basement of an old church at Ninth and Grand, and it was one big room. They had blankets available for people who wanted to sleep on the floor, snacks, and all the coffee a person could want. The majority of the people staying there would sit up all night watching TV, playing cards, talking, or just doing whatever. It was mainly a place where people could get in out of the cold to keep from freezing.

I became friends with the director of the new shelter that later became known as Restart, and after I'd stayed there for a couple nights, he asked me if I would like to be on the shelter's staff. Naturally, I accepted. I didn't accept because I wanted to help others. I accepted because being on staff meant that I wouldn't be put out of the place at five in the morning like the majority of the people staying there.

I would have a place to take a shower, a place to eat meals, and a place to sleep during the day. Taking the staff position seemed like an answer to my problems. In the days before I gave the dogs away, I was also able to return to the trailer and feed them each day.

This was how I became a member of the original staff of what ended up being the Restart shelter. The reason the director had asked me to join the staff was because I had a gift. I was able to talk people into donating materials to the shelter. He once told me that we needed coffee. I got on the phone and found someone to donate a couple of cases of coffee. I was able to talk people into donating just about anything the director wanted—from materials to cash.

The majority of the other staff members had also been homeless when they became members, of Restart and just like the homeless on the streets, went by nicknames. The head staff member went by his real name, John, but the others had nicknames like Dog and St. Louis. Of course, everybody called me Tripp.

There were seven or eight of us on the staff there. We were a mixture of many different attitudes, and each of us had our own story for being there. Take Dog, for instance; his story was that he was a carnie who had lost his job for the winter. That's how he ended up at that shelter one night. St. Louis had gotten a divorce and lost everything he'd had in Kansas City—his wife, his kids, and his house. By the time his wife's lawyer had finished with him, he was left with only the shirt on his back. Two Feathers was an old Indian who had gotten tired of the reservation. He'd been searching for a new life when he ended up on the streets of Kansas City. Most would think of this group as a bunch of misfits, and I might agree, but there in the basement of that church, we became a family. For the most part, we were also a group of caring people.

It was at this place where I had my experience with the boy and his piggy bank. This is where God taught me about compassion for my brothers and sisters. It's also where he changed my heart from just caring about myself to caring about others. It was there that I started my mission of making a difference for others. And truthfully, it was there that I started meeting different factions of the community. This was necessary, because I needed to start making plans for my future. Part of my plan required that I network with people in the community who were making a difference.

It took time for us to really get to know each other. By the time I left that shelter, I knew a lot of their stories. We would discuss our personal lives as if we were related. The talk usually centered around the clients that came in on any given night, but there were moments when someone on staff would relate a personal story. Take Dog, for instance. He would talk about his carnie days. He'd tell us how they used to get a girlfriend and then get rid of her when they got tired of her by passing her on to some other carnie that ran a different ride. Or Two Feathers would tell stories about living on the reservation and how the government had cheated the Indians out of their land and heritage over the years.

We also discussed other people and other programs that were truly making a difference for the homeless in our community.

The Real Deal

I mentioned the Homeless Information Center earlier, but I'll go into a little more detail about the place now. After the Restart shelter closed its doors for the winter it was the Homeless Information Center that became my operation base for a few years. This is where I held my first Christmas Breakfast for the Homeless in 1990. It's also the place I held my first board meeting, put our first board together, and was granted 501(c)(3) nonprofit status. It's literally the place where COPP was born, and I'll never forget the first time I walked though the door. The center had been started by "Legal Aid" of Kansas City, but then it was taken over by Metropolitan Lutheran Ministries

Like most places that help the poor and homeless, the Homeless Information Center ended up being run by a religious group to make a difference for those hurting in the community. This particular center was then run by the Metropolitan Lutheran Ministries (or MLM, as they are known in our community), and for a long time, for years as a matter of fact, they were about the best operation the poor and homeless of our community had going for them.

When I walked into the center in 1989, it was a place where a person could count on getting help if they really wanted it. The center provided everything. You could use their phone to try to get a job interview, take a shower, or wash your clothes. And people seeking to get their lives back on track were given a case manager who would really try to help them straighten things out.

Some of the other services they offered included helping people obtain their state ID and getting people signed up for food stamps by providing them with an address they could use to receive mail. (At that time, you couldn't receive food stamps without a mailing address.) It was place where the staff members truly seemed to care about the clients. There were a few paid staff members. The others were volunteers, most of them homeless themselves.

I knew about the center via word of mouth. However, I never really checked it out. I'd stopped in the day after I'd sought refuge from the cold at the police station. It was a couple of weeks later before I went back to find out what the center really offered. To say the least, I was impressed by their menu of services. They even had footlockers where you could store your belongings.

The center was housed in an old storefront building that had been converted into what was more or less a day center for the homeless. It was one long room, and in front there was an office. Next to it was a kitchen, and in the very back of the room there was a door which led to the shower, a washing machine, and a dryer. As soon as someone walked through the front door, there was a desk where they could fill out a form about what help they might need. Then the staff person manning the desk would take the form to the director of the center. This person acted more like a case manager than a director of operations.

He would call the person into his office and try to help them with whatever they needed. He'd explain the center's capabilities and services they might be able to provide. The director's name was Ken West, and the one thing you could tell about him up front was that he cared about the people he was helping. With him, you weren't a number. You were human. He helped a lot of brothers and sisters get back on their feet during the years he spent at the Homeless Information Center.

He also had a couple of other paid staff members there who were just as dedicated as he was. One was a woman named Jennie Wells. Besides being a paid staff member of Metropolitan Lutheran Ministries, she went around with her husband at night and fed the homeless at their camps. She also had a program she worked on at night where she helped feed and clothe homeless veterans. A lot of the materials she would give out were donated by the Veterans of Foreign Wars organization. She wasn't paid to feed the homeless and the vets. As a matter of fact, she spent a lot of her wages feeding these people.

Another staff member I would like to tell you about was a volunteer at the center. Her name was Lucille, and she was the one who helped people do laundry. She was a big lady. As I remember, she weighed about three hundred pounds. When I first met her, she was already in her sixties. No matter how bad the weather was or how bad Lucille was feeling, she was always there for those hurting. She had a heart twice the size of her body, and she would do anything she could to help a person in need. She was the mother many of the homeless never had. She treated these people with love and compassion no matter their race, creed, or religion. When she passed away, I know she went to be with Jesus. She showed his love and compassion to hundreds of people while she was here on earth.

By the time I made my way to the Homeless Information Center to check the organization out, I had heard a lot of stories about them from different homeless brothers and sisters. These friends had raved about the assistance a person could get at the center. Of course, talk is cheap, and I had learned by that time that the only way to really find out the truth about something was to check it out.

One of the stories I had heard was that the staff at the center had helped a couple of guys get their Social Security benefits. I knew my time on the staff at the Restart shelter would soon be up. I was hoping the staff at the center might be able to help me get some money coming in from Social Security.

I walked in the front door and walked up to the reception desk. The staff member on duty at the time asked me what I needed. I told her, and she gave me a card to fill out. The card asked a lot of personal questions, and at first I was reluctant to fill it out. They wanted to know information like my Social Security number and my mother's maiden name. I asked the receptionist why they needed that information. She assured me that they didn't give the information out to anybody; it was just for their files. With her assurance, I filled out the card and handed it back to her.

She told me to have a seat with the other clients who were there while she took my card back to Mr. West.

"Oh, by the way," she said, "feel free to get yourself a cup of coffee and a donut while you're waiting."

I did so and sat down with a bunch of other homeless clients. After a while, the receptionist called my name and said, "Mr. West will see you now, Mr. Tripp."

I walked into his office and got my first look at Ken West. He was an African American about six feet tall and weighed about one hundred fifty pounds. He was not the only person in the room, though. There was another African American gentleman that introduced himself as Ronald Casanova, a coworker of Mr. West's. Ron Casanova was a smaller, short, stocky, black gentleman who weighed a few pounds more that Mr. West even though he was a lot shorter.

Mr. West said, "Please have a seat, Mr. Tripp. How can we help you today?"

"Well, I heard this place could help me get my Social Security started," I replied.

"Well, we have helped some. Actually we have a legal aid lawyer who comes in a couple days a week and helps people get their Social Security income, but it takes a while to get it started. What other problems do you have that we might be able to help you with?"

For some reason, I felt at ease with him, and I started telling him my problems. I told him everything, from how I'd ended up homeless to the problems I'd gotten myself into with the shelters. He seemed really concerned when I was finished. He said, "Well, for starters, we can set you up with an appointment to see the legal aid lawyer."

He also told me that if I needed them, he could give me a set of clean clothes from their clothing room.

"Are you drawing your food stamps?" he asked.

"Yes, I already get them."

"When's the last time you saw a doctor?" he asked.

"A few months ago. Why?"

He said. "Well, we could set you up to see the doctor that comes here every week from the Swope Parkway Health Center. They treat the homeless for free."

"That sounds good to me," I replied. "Set me up. By the way, Mr. West, would you happen to have any shoes in your clothing room?"

"I'm not sure. I'll have Mr. Casanova check for you."

With that he said, "Well, that's all we can do for now. If any additional problems come up, you know where we are."

He told me he would set up appointments for me with the lawyer and the doctor. He then asked that I have a seat back in the waiting room while Mr. Casanova looked to see if they had any shoes in my size.

When I left that center that day I had a new pair of shoes on my feet, and I knew I had met someone who was the real deal.

Information Center Indeed

I had moved back to my camp at the trailer and had left the post I'd held on the Restart staff. I left my post because even though me and the director of that shelter were friends I didn't see eye to eye with the way he was running some of his programs at the shelter. I did not approve of what some of the other staff members were doing, or how they were treating some of the homeless brothers and sisters less than human, like they were trash. Another problem was that I was soliciting donated materials for the homeless, but the materials weren't making it into their hands. The preacher and I had several heated arguments about that before I left. One of the arguments was over popcorn, of all things. You see, I had been getting on the phone and convincing different companies to donate foodstuffs to the shelter. The different companies were coming through and donating the materials we needed, but sometimes staff members were grabbing stuff—like five-gallon tins of different flavored popcorn—for themselves. A company was donating the tins of popcorn to the homeless, and certain members of the staff were taking them out and selling them on the street. Eventually, word got back to this particular popcorn company, and they stopped donating to the shelter because of it. Of course, I was the one who looked bad in the deal, because I was the one who had told the donors that their donations would be used to feed the homeless. I never mentioned that their charitable donation might actually end up being peddled on the street by greedy staff members. This misuse of donations was only one of the reasons I left, but it was enough. You see, when I give my word, I keep it.

After that first meeting with Ken West, I started spending as much time at the center as I could. As a matter of fact, over time we became good friends. The same was true of Ron Casanova. Ken was a wealth of information about how to form a 501(c)(3) nonprofit organization. He also knew just about every director of every shelter and program that dealt with homelessness in Kansas City, and he knew how they operated their various organizations.

Ronald "Cass" Casanova, on the other hand, was a homeless activist from New York. He had been involved in the takeover of abandoned housing by the poor and homeless people of New York City, and he liked to tell stories about it. I listened to his stories and never complained about his constant chatter, because I was amazed at how much he had accomplished in New York and other cities. I was also amazed by some of the things he'd gotten away with. I wanted to take in all the information both Cass and West were willing to share, because I knew that eventually I was going do something about the way the homeless and poor were being treated in Kansas City.

There was always someone stopping in at the center who was in the know about things going on in our city. Ministers stopped in; the media wanted to do stories about the center; politicians dropped by. I decided that the Homeless Information Center was an ideal place to learn as much as I could about a little of everything. I started volunteering to work the reception desk at the center in my spare time. It was a way of remaining in the know. Besides that, it provided me with a list of friends and contacts inside the various organizations. These people would fill me in on what was happening in their particular realm, and my homeless brothers and sisters kept me informed of anything they heard.

You might say I was working undercover. It was a deep cover, because no one, including myself, really knew what I had planned. I knew that an idea would come to me eventually, and when that opportunity presented itself, I wanted to be prepared. One thing I learned early on from Cass was that he operated with the help of the media. I think he made sure that anything he had a hand in was covered by the media. It was a lesson I would learn very well. If used correctly, the pen can be stronger than just about anything else. If you can get the public's attention and the cause is just, then you have the battle half won. Of course, you have to figure out what story you want the media to print. Then you have to manipulate the media into printing your version of that story. I started writing stories about different things that were going on with the homeless here in our city. I would send them to little rag newspapers here in town, and eventually they began showing up in print. Of course, I used a different name, but I must have written some good stories, because they started showing up.

As my confidence grew, I decided I might as well go for broke and send letters to each of the city's councilmen. I wanted to let them know what was really going on with the homeless population in our town. The difference between the letters and the newspaper articles was that I used my real name on the letters. In hindsight, I'm pretty sure the councilmen may have thought I was some kind of kook. Not one of them ever contacted me.

I had been doing volunteer work at the center for a month or two when my big idea finally started to form. It was a couple of weeks before Christmas when the opportunity I'd been waiting for showed up. I was going to make a positive impact on the poor and homeless. I had a gut feeling that if I got this story out to the public, it would be the start of something big. My idea would not only help the poor, but it would put my name out there, and maybe, just maybe, it would give me the platform I needed to launch my own organization—an organization that would really make a difference for those who were hurting.

Every shelter and organization in town held Christmas celebrations for the poor and homeless, but then every one of them would put these same people—men, women, and children—out on the street come Christmas morning. This was supposedly done so the shelters and organizations could get Christmas dinner prepared.

The problem was that there was nowhere for these people to go on Christmas morning. Nothing was open except maybe hospital emergency rooms, and they would run the transients out. The library and everything else was closed. Homeless men, women, and children found Christmas morning very difficult.

This Christmas morning problem was the dilemma I'd set out to resolve, and with some cooperation from Ken and Cass, I believed I'd come up with a solution. If I could talk Ken and Cass into opening the homeless center on Christmas morning, then my plan would have wings. However, the men wouldn't be being paid to do this, and Ken would have to get his organization, Metropolitan Lutheran Ministries, to give him permission to open the building whether he got paid or not. I went to work on Ron and Cass, telling them the solution I had come up with.

When I presented the idea to them, they said they would think about it and let me know what they'd decided by the end of the week. They also asked a lot of questions. They mainly wanted to know what we were going do with at least several hundred people for three to four hours while we waited for the shelters and other organizations to reopen for Christmas dinner.

I told Ron and Cass that if they would open center, I would figure out how we would take care of the people. My main concern was getting them off the streets on Christmas morning. The secondary problem would be what to do with them, but my whole plan would only work if I had the building open for them. So the building was the key, and you had better believe I did a lot of praying that week. And thanks to a phone call I made I got my answer the next week.

Not a Dumb Cab Driver

That night as I left the center, I kept asking myself, "How am I going to make this event happen?" I also wondered what we could to do with all those people for the three or four hours they'd be at the center. I mean, it would be five in the morning when they were released from the shelters. What could I do with them in the center from six o'clock until the shelters and organizations started opening up to serve Christmas dinner? The obvious answer would be to give them something to eat, and maybe set up a TV and show a Christmas movie or cartoons so the kids would have something to do.

The problem, aside from not having permission to open the center on Christmas morning, was that I didn't have any of that stuff. I began to wonder how I could acquire the things I was going to need. Then the answer sort of just came to me. When I'd been at the Restart shelter I'd used their phones to solicit donations for the shelter. I could do the same in this situation, to get the materials for the Christmas morning. Of course, another problem was that I didn't have much time to pull this off. The first thing I did the next morning when I arrived at the center was ask Ken if it would be okay if I used the phone that day to try to get some materials donated for the event.

He agreed to it, but also reminded me, "You know we still haven't said yes to the event, and we don't have the green light from Metropolitan Lutheran Ministries to open up on Christmas."

I replied, "Don't worry, you will," as I left his office.

But he was right. How could I make sure Metropolitan Lutheran Ministries would agree to open the building? I decided it might help if I could find a way to put some pressure on them to say yes. What better way to do this than to feed the newspaper a story about the problem and how the Homeless Information Center was going to solve it.

Like I said, I had learned a lot from Cass. It was time for me to put my own flare on it in my city. So that is exactly what I did. I called the *Kansas City Star* and leaked the story about the problem the homeless were facing. I also fed them a line that indicated that the Metropolitan Lutheran Ministries was opening its doors to these people on Christmas morning out of the goodness of its heart. What can I say? It was a human interest story the paper could really get behind. It was also a story that would make Metropolitan Lutheran Ministries and the homeless center look good to the public.

I would have really loved being a fly on the wall when their director got the call from the *Star* for a comment on the story. Since the *Star* had been fed the truth on the problem by yours truly, how would it look to the paper or the public if the story got that far and then Metropolitan Lutheran Ministries said it had no knowledge of the problem or the event? Yes, it was a big gamble on my part, but one that I thought I had to take in order to make things happen.

After I called the newspaper, I started calling places in search of food donations for Christmas morning. One of the places I called was a bakery, Lamar's Donuts. The owner, Ray Lamar, was a man who cared about his community. I had used him before to donate donuts to another shelter where I had been on staff.

I got him on the phone and told him what I had planned.

He said, "Would a hundred dozen be enough?"

I was shocked and said, "Yes, it would."

He said, "Well, you can pick them up at my place on Christmas Eve."

I thanked him and let him go.

The next call I made was to a coffee company; they donated a case of coffee. Things seemed to be going well. I had coffee and donuts after just a few minutes on the phone.

About that time, I was interrupted by Ken; he said, "Mr. Tripp, I would like to speak to you in my office."

I walked into his office and had a seat. He sat down at his desk and just stared at me for a few seconds before he spoke.

"I just had a talk with my boss. He asked me what was going on down here. By the way, he said a newspaper had just called him and asked him about the event we're planning to host for the homeless on Christmas morning. He also asked me why I hadn't informed him about it. I might add that he wasn't happy. Would you happen to know anything about a reporter at the newspaper getting a story about something going on at our center?"

"Well, Ken, maybe someone heard us talking about it or something," I replied.

"I don't believe that for one second," he replied. "But I'll tell you this, if you ever go over my head like this again, you won't be volunteering here anymore."

Once the threat was past his lips he sort of smiled and said, "By the way, the director at Metropolitan Lutheran Ministries said we could open up on Christmas morning. So I guess we'll be having that event."

"Praise Jesus," I said.

"By the way," he added, "there is supposed to be a reporter from the *Star* down here after a while to do a story and to see what materials we might need for the event."

As I left his office to get back to working on the phone, I knew I hadn't fooled Ron with the story of someone else speaking to the *Star*. At the same time, I had a feeling he was starting to figure out that I wasn't thc dumb cab driver I tried to make people believe I was. The wheels in my mind were turning. I was already carefully planning what I would say to the reporter, and I was making a mental list of things I might ask the public to donate. After all, it was only a few short days before Christmas.

Later that day, the reporter arrived, approached the reception desk, identified himself, and asked to speak to Mr. West. I knocked on Ken's office door and let him know the reporter from the *Star* was there.

Ken came out after a minute or two and invited the reporter into his office. After about ten minutes or so the intercom rang, and Ken said, "Mr. Tripp, would you please come into my office?"

I walked in, and Ken introduced me to the reporter. Ken said, "This is Mr. Tripp, the homeless gentleman we have been talking about."

The reporter shook my hand and said, "So you're the person setting up this event."

"Well, I'm just helping," I said.

"What do you expect to do?" he asked.

"We're just trying to give the poor and homeless a place where they can go on Christmas morning," I replied.

"Well, Mr. West has told me part of your plans. How do you think our readers might be able to help you?"

"Well, we could use some donated food, and it would be nice if people could donate some gifts that we could hand out on Christmas morning. Maybe the public could donate presents, like toys for the kids and maybe gloves, warm clothing, and hygiene articles for the grownups."

"Have you got enough room to cook for that many?"

"Well, no, but I was thinking of foodstuffs like fresh fruit and maybe cereal. We do have some coffee and donuts donated already."

"Oh really, who donated those?"

I told him, and then he said, "I'll do a story and see if we can get you some more donations." He then asked, "Where can our readers contact you?"

"Here at the center," I replied, as I rattled off the center's phone number. "Just have them call us here."

"Well, I'll have a story in the paper in the morning. Maybe we can help you with your project."

"By the way, Mr. Tripp, how will you let the homeless know that you'll be opening up this building on Christmas?"

"Mostly by word of mouth. It doesn't take long for the information to get out to the homeless."

With that the interview was over, and I left the office. That night I found it hard to sleep. I was wondering if the public would respond when they read the story. The next morning, I found out.

Response

The next morning I headed for Mickey D's, as I did every morning. When I got there, Abe and Pockets were already at a table. Abe had a copy of the Kansas City Star morning newspaper in his hand, and he said to me, "Tripp, you did it again. There's a story in this paper about the homeless center, and you're in it. I didn't know you were planning something for us on Christmas morning."

"Well, Abe, there's a lot you don't know about me," I said as I laughed.

About that time, Pockets added, "You know, if you keep this up, Tripp, you might make a lot of friends."

"I know, Pockets, but at the same time I might make a lot of enemies. Anyway, Abe let me see that article."

He handed it to me, and I read it. I was amazed. The reporter had really done a good job of getting the facts out.

I said, "Abe, do you think this article will do any good?"

He said, "Well, who knows what the public will do."

Abe was right. So we continued to speculate about what might happen, until it was time for Abe and Pockets to head to the labor pool and time for me to head to the center.

When I got there, I saw thirty to forty homeless people standing in line in front of the center waiting for it to open. One of them saw me walking up the street toward the center and yelled out, "Here comes Tripp."

About that time a group of people ran toward me. I didn't know what was going on, but I found out soon enough. They were all asking me questions about Christmas morning. They wanted to know, "What are you going to have?" and "What time are you going to open?" I guess one or more of them had read the article in the paper that morning; the news had spread like wildfire.

I said, "Just be here, and you'll find out."

I then added, "Just tell everyone you know we'll be open," and I left it at that.

When I got to the door, Ken let me in and said, "How are we today, Mr. Tripp?"

"Okay, I guess. I sure didn't expect the welcome I got outside."

"Well, you'd better get used to it. I read that article this morning, and I think you're going to be one popular guy for the next couple of days," he replied, "not only with our clients but also with the public."

I smiled. He didn't know it, at least I don't think he knew it, but that's what I was counting on. I sat down at the reception desk and started signing people in when Ken opened the door. About that time, the phone started ringing. Everybody was asking to speak to me. As soon as I would finish a conversation and hang up with one caller, another call would come in. People wanted to know what we needed for the Christmas event, and they wanted to know where they could drop off donations. The influx of calls became so intense that I had to ask Ken to put someone else on the desk so I could go to the back room and answer calls. I had expected some calls from people wanting to help, but I had never dreamed the event would draw this kind of response from the public.

And then the donations started coming in. You name it, it got it dropped off at the center. We got food, warm clothes, stuffed toys, gloves, hats, hygiene items, and so on. Naturally, I kept a notebook for myself where I wrote down the name of every person who brought a donation to the center. I also wrote down their phone numbers and their addresses. I would eventually send each of them a note of thanks. Of course, that wasn't my only reason for recording the information. I was also smart enough to know I might be able to solicit some of them for help again, if and when I got my organization going. I was basically developing a mailing list.

After seeing the outpouring of love, compassion, and generosity by the people who made donations to our first Christmas event, I knew the formation of my organization was more a matter of *when*, not *if*. By the time the center closed for the evening and I'd walked back to my camp, I was worn out. But I knew it had been a good day. I knew that the article the reporter had done had touched a lot of people's hearts, and it looked like the poor and homeless brothers and sisters were going to have a spectacular Christmas morning. I assure you, I didn't have any problem getting to sleep that evening.

The next few days were filled with phone calls, donations, and figuring out just how we were going to hand out the donations and organize events on Christmas morning. Then, before I knew it, it *was* Christmas morning, and it was time for the event. Believe it or not, the phone calls and donations kept coming right up to and including Christmas morning.

Christmas for Everyone

It was Christmas Eve, and I'd talked Ken into letting me stay in the building after the center closed. I wanted to change the room around, put up a Christmas tree, and decorate before the morning of the event. The tree, complete with lights and trimming, had been among the many donations the center had received that week. Ken and Cass stuck with me at the center until about ten o'clock.

After that, they locked me in and went on with their lives. It was going to be a long night, and I had plenty to do to keep me busy. Ken had picked up the donuts from Lamar's earlier in the evening, so I had something to snack on. Putting up the tree was hard, because it was so big that the top of it went clear to the ceiling. I had to remove a part of the ceiling tile just to put the tree's top decoration on. After I got the tree done, I started putting the kids' gifts—the stuffed animals and toys—around it. Naturally, this made me think of my own kids. They'd always been ready for Santa Claus when they were little.

In a way, I was sad thinking about not being with my kids that night, but in another way, I knew there would be a lot of homeless kids in that center in the morning. I was quite sure those kids would have the same looks on their faces that mine used to get when they were little. The thought made me feel better. But, like everyone, I longed to be with my family on Christmas. At the same time, I had a job to do, and I was going see it through. I mean, I could have found some way to get to my parents' house or to one of my kids' houses and spent Christmas with some family. But if I'd have done that, there would be no Christmas event at the center. In my mind's eye, I kept seeing women and children being put out of the shelters and into the cold on Christmas morning, and I knew I had to do something about it. So there I was, arranging donated stuffed animals around a donated tree.

The next thing I needed to do was set up a line of tables to put food on. I might add that we'd received a ton of donated food—fresh fruit juice, cold cereal, pastries, donuts, and coffee. We'd also taken in enough gloves, scarves, socks, and so on that we were going to be able to give the adults gifts. Finally, I set up the chairs in the back of the room. I also set up the TV and the VCR that Ken had talked Metropolitan Lutheran Ministries into letting us use for the Christmas celebration. By the time I was done, it was about three in the morning. I decided to lie down on a pallet I'd made on the floor to get a little rest before people started arriving for the Christmas Breakfast for the Homeless.

The next thing I remember is hearing my name, "Tripp, Tripp, you okay?"

I said, "I guess."

It was Ken. He had come in, and I guess I was really sleeping well.

"What time is it?" I asked

He replied, "It's about four."

"I must have fallen asleep," I said. "What're you doing here so early, Ken?"

"I just thought I'd come down and see if you had everything ready," he said after he walked around looking at the decorations, the tree, and the toys around it. "You sure have a lot of nice toys for the kids," he added.

"Yes, the public really came through. I guess it's as ready as it's going to get. There are supposed to be some volunteers coming down about five thirty to help serve."

"Okay, Mr. Tripp," Ken said, "I'm going to my office. It's your show."

With that he went into his office. To tell the truth, I don't remember seeing him again until the event was almost over. I got up, put my blankets away, and started the coffeepots going with fresh coffee. By the time I was finished with that, there was a knock on the door. It was some of the volunteers.

"We're ready to help you do whatever needs to be done, Mr. Tripp," one of the volunteers said.

I said, "Well, it will be a while before the homeless start showing up. Why don't you all have some coffee or a donut while you wait?"

It wasn't long before other volunteers started showing up, so I started giving them jobs to do. One of the neat things that morning was that some of the volunteers were bringing their children to help on the serving line. We also used some of them to help us pass out gifts.

At about quarter after six, the homeless started showing up—men, women, and children. Before everything was over at eleven o'clock, we had that building packed with people, and everybody—the homeless and the volunteers—were having a good time. As a matter of fact, if you hadn't known better, you would have sworn they were all just one, big family having fun together. I think the volunteers were surprised by how much the homeless appreciated what the volunteers had done for them.

I saw many tears of joy that morning, not only from the homeless but also from the volunteers. I was touched by the looks on the faces of the homeless children when they walked through the door and saw the Christmas tree with all of the gifts under it.

To keep order, I had to tell everybody that the toys wouldn't be handed out until about nine o'clock. That way I felt each kid would have an equal chance of getting the toy they wanted.

The one problem I had was that some of the homeless wanted to grab the toys when they came in the door. Unfortunately, like everything in life, you'll always have those who are constantly looking for a way to make a quick buck. The people who pestered me about the toys didn't even have any kids with them, but they each had an excuse as to why they should get to have the toys. I had to put my foot down and tell them all that none of the toys would be touched until each child present at the breakfast had gotten one. If there were any leftovers, the adults who were there without kids would be allowed to have some at that time.

Needless to say, I wasn't at the top of some of those people's most-liked list after I made that ruling. When you get that many people in one place, there are bound to be a few who aren't happy with the rules. But I did what I thought was right, and I'd do it again. At about nine o'clock or so, we let the kids get their toys. Several people videotaped the children as they received their gifts; the awe in their eyes, the smiles on their faces, and their joyous reactions were priceless. It was a lot of fun to watch little kids go for the biggest stuffed toys; sometimes the toy was actually bigger than the child. When the kids were done, we let the grownups have what was left. There were long johns, underwear, socks, and gloves for all.

By then it was time to end the event so people could head off to various shelters for their Christmas dinners and celebrations. When it was all over, I was exhausted. But I was happy because so many people had been helped. I had been able to bring those that *had* together with those in *need*, and those that *had* actually got to see where their donations went. Everybody had a good time.

The newspaper showed up and did a story about the event, and yes, my name got out there. But more importantly, the story in the paper showed the public that it was a lot of fun getting involved in the event on a personal level. Getting involved was even more important than writing a check. I'm not saying that the checks aren't important. Let me put it this way. If you go to the store to buy a loaf of bread, you expect to get the quality you pay for. Why should it be any different when you write a check to an organization? You should know where your money is actually going. The best way to know for sure is to be there.

Aftermath

For several weeks after the event, I was the talk of the town. The reporter for the *Kansas City Star* newspaper had done a wonderful job in spreading the word about the event and about the homeless man who had started the event, namely me. So the name Richard Tripp was starting to be recognized by the public.

I, on the other hand, was wondering what I should do or what I could do to keep the public's attention on the problem of the poor and homeless in our community. The holidays were over, and after the holidays, the average person forgets about the problems others are facing. I can understand it. The bills need to be paid after the holidays, and sometimes it's hard to think about others when the wolf is at your door. That's why most not-for-profits organize the bulk of their fund-raising during the holidays. That's when the public's attention is most attuned to the problems of the homeless and poor. But like I said, the public's attention span only lasts so long. You have to keep reminding them of the problems in your community. Unfortunately, the problems the poor and homeless face don't stop after the holidays. As a matter of fact, if anything, their problems usually get worse, especially if the weather is bad.

On December 26, I was sitting at my desk at the homeless center running all kinds of ideas around in my mind. I had to do a lot of personal soul-searching as I thought about what my next step should be. I asked myself a lot of questions. Yes, I had done a good thing with the event, but that had been yesterday. What about today? Not to mention tomorrow. Just how far or how committed to the down-and-out did I want to become?

I couldn't just sit at the center every day. While it was cozy having somewhere to get in out of the cold, and I was learning a lot about the needs of others, I still had needs of my own, and I knew that in order to help others, I had to first help myself. That meant I needed to figure out a way to support myself. I needed to come in off the street and get back to work.

The numbness in my legs had stopped, and I figured the only thing I could do was try to go back to work driving a cab. The legal aid lawyer I had spoken with told me that it could take years to get my SSI benefits, and I didn't want to be homeless that long. I would have to figure out a way of not only getting back to work but also paying for my hack license. Not to mention, I had a problem with an old warrant for not paying a DWI fine that I had gotten a year or so before I became homeless.

I had no idea how much money or what kind of hoops I was going to have to jump through to get my driver's license back. But I knew I couldn't help many people if I simply sat behind that desk. I needed to come up with a plan to help myself before I worried about helping others. In the meantime, I would be at the desk trying to help those poor souls that ended up coming through the doors of this center.

So, I set out to get the money it would take to get my life back together. I asked Ken if he knew anyone who might help me take care of my financial problems. But he didn't really know of any organizations that would help me with financial support.

Oddly enough, the help came from the last place in the world I would've expected it. I was sitting at the desk of the homeless center one day when an old friend I hadn't seen in a few months came in to see Ken. It was Abe. The reason I hadn't seen him was because he had gotten off the streets and was living somewhere over in Kansas City, Kansas. After a couple of years on the streets, he had finally gotten his SSI benefits started. I had wondered why he had dropped out of sight. Now I knew.

After he was done talking with Ken, I said, "Hey, Abe, where've you been?"

He replied, "I'm living over in Kansas. I have my own place now. If you want, I'll wait till the center closes and you can come see my place, Tripp. Maybe you can have dinner with me and Amanda. She's living with me."

"You've got to be kidding," I said.

"Nope, we started living together last month."

"Okay, Abe, stick around for a few minutes. We'll be closing soon, and I'll spend the night with you guys."

"Sounds good," he said.

Across the street from the homeless center, there was a restaurant called Tom's. When we had money, and when we didn't end up at Mickey D's, we would go to Tom's for coffee in the morning before the center opened. It was the cheapest restaurant in town, and it was in a building that housed Section 8 apartments. A lot of the people living in those apartments would come down in the morning to have coffee. I had met Amanda for the first time one morning at Tom's. Pockets, Abe, and I had gone there one morning for coffee. I was kind of surprised she had moved in with Abe. I mean, she was on SSI payments too, so I guess it was a good match for both of them since they had two incomes rather than one. But to tell you the truth, I thought she had the hots for me back then. She would always buy me coffee on the mornings when she thought I didn't have the money for it. The only problem was that she was a lot older than I was, and I wasn't interested in anything but friendship. Actually, the truth is that I only talked to her to get free coffee. Anyway, I was happy that she and Abe had gotten together. They were more compatible in age than we would have been.

I went with Abe that night and spent the night at their place. Over dinner we talked about my plans for the future, and I explained to them the problems I was having. We played rummy most of the night and then went to bed. The next morning, we got up late and had coffee. I was getting ready to head back to the homeless center when Abe said, "Tripp, me and Amanda had a thought last night."

"Oh really, what was that, Abe?" I asked.

"Well, it's like this. We both have to use a cab a lot to go to our doctors and stuff, so suppose we make a deal."

"What kind of deal, Abe?"

"If we loan you the money to take care of your problems and get you back to work, would you be able to run us on a couple of errands each week for, say, the next year?"

"Well, hell yes," I replied.

"Well, consider it done then. Just let us know how much it takes to get everything done, and we'll write you a check." I couldn't believe it. Was this for real?

Not Ready to Make Nice

I was sitting at the reception desk at the homeless center. Parked outside was my taxi; I had the keys in my hand. Abe and Amanda had come through with the money for me to get back on my feet. I understand that most people probably would have just walked off and went on with their life once they got a chance to get back on their feet. The difference was that I wasn't most people. I couldn't just forget all the hurt and injustice I had seen piled on my poor and homeless brothers and sisters, not to mention what I had gone through that year I'd spent on the street.

What these keys in my hand gave me was my own brand of justice, so to speak. They gave me the ability to take on the systems that be, and to do it without worrying that I might get caught with my pants down. As long as I had wheels, I couldn't be stopped. I didn't have to worry about someone catching me at my camp and hurting me; I no longer worried that a gang of thugs sent by one of the shelters was waiting around every corner. What the keys gave me was the freedom to wage war on the systems that be, to change the way they treated the poor and homeless.

I hadn't forgotten the abuses and needless deaths I had seen my brothers and sisters endure just because they were down. I was tired and fed up with the majority of the systems. They would push Jesus Christ and heaven up front, and then treat the people like Lucifer. The system was broken, and I was going to try to fix it, or at least I was going to try to make sure people got treated like human beings. I guess you could say I definitely wasn't ready to "make nice" with the system. I knew at that moment that what I was getting ready to do would bring out the truth about the system, and the public would have their eyes opened like never before.

They say the truth will set you free, and I was ready to let the truth out. I wanted the public to know that it wasn't just one shelter or one organization that was doing damage to the poor and homeless. They all had a hand in it, and they would all cover for each other. I was aware that I was putting my life on the line, and I also realized that sometime during this war I might lose it by being a threat to those not wanting the truth to get out about the conditions the homeless were having to face. Believe me, ladies and gentlemen, there was no doubt my fight would feel like a war, and once I opened Pandora's Box, I would not be able to back out of the fight, not that I would want to. My spirit would not allow me to sit idly by and continue to watch people being treated as less than human.

I was tired of seeing men freeze their toes and fingers off, just because they didn't have a dollar to give the shelter operators, or because they might have had the smell of alcohol on their breath. I'll never forget an old man that came into the homeless center one day. He had been beaten up, and his Social Security money had been stolen. I talked him into going to one of the shelters for the weekend, until he could get his relatives to send him some money on Monday so he could buy a bus ticket and go home. That Monday morning, I found out that the old man had done what I told him to do, and I'm sorry to say that he sat in that shelter's TV room on Sunday night and hemorrhaged to death. Nobody at the shelter even bothered to call for help. They just let him sit in the chair and die. I'm not saying they could have made a big difference, but at least if someone had called an ambulance, the man might have had a chance.

Another incident involves a gentleman who smelled of alcohol when he tried to check into a Kansas City shelter. The staff member working registration that night decided that the man had been drinking and denied him access to the shelter that night. The temperature was in the low teens, and instead of allowing the man access to the shelter, they let him sit outside for hours before they decided to let him in. Needless to say, by the time they brought the man inside, he had severe frostbite to his fingers and toes. After a while, the staff decided that the man needed medical attention. They did call an ambulance for him, but they'd waited too long. The man had to have several of his fingers and toes removed all because one staff member, a person who probably never had training on how to handle situations like that, decided he was God. That staff member had made the decision that the man had been drinking, and the staff member denied him access to a warm bed. I was told by several of my homeless brothers on the streets that this particular shelter thought that they might be sued, or a reporter might get a hold of the story, so they fired the staff member responsible for the incident.

By that time, I was tired of seeing those that had a little power use their influence to sexually abuse the men, women, and children that needed help in the system. I admit I wasn't God, and to some it might seem like I was trying to be, but the fact of the matter was that too many were being hurt to let the systems continue the way they were. Someone somewhere had to step up to the plate, and it looked to me like I was the only one who dared try. Nobody else would put their life on the line. They knew what was going on, but they feared repercussions.

Was I scared? Yes, I was. But I will be a lot more scared the day I meet Jesus and he asks me why I didn't help those who were being used, those in need, and those who were being abused by the very system that uses his name to do so much harm. You see, I believe in walking Jesus, not just talking Jesus. I might add that I fully expected God, his son Jesus Christ, and the Holy Sprit to see me through all the battles and wars I was about to face.

Devising a Plan

Since the day I had walked into that first shelter and saw the way people were being treated, I had been planning a way to make a difference. I didn't really know how I was going to do it, but I knew that eventually I would get it done. All they'd managed to do when they kicked me out in the cold at that second shelter was make me more determined to make a difference for those who were being abused. All along, I had watched their every move and done everything I could to learn their methods of doing things and, I might add, their vulnerabilities. Now I was going to use those to the max. I had learned a lot from Cass and Ken. I also had become friends with a lot of people who worked at the different shelters, and I had learned a lot from them also.

One major vulnerability had been holding me back. That vulnerability was that I was stuck traveling on foot, and now even that had been taken care of.

It's funny how the public reacts when it thinks it's been duped by an organization. The donations seem to dry up until the public thinks the problem has been fixed. What most people don't understand is homelessness is big business with a lot of money. We're talking millions of dollars being funneled into the different organizations. Unfortunately, the money doesn't always make it to those in need; and no matter how much is given, it doesn't seem to make much of a difference. I'm not just talking about shelters. I'm talking about the whole gamut of those having anything to do with the poor or homeless. That's why I am so vocal when urging people who donate to the poor to get personally involved and see where every cent goes.

I knew that I had to walk a fine line in whatever I did. I knew that if too much of the truth was put out to the public, then the public might stop supporting certain organizations completely. And although I personally thought that might not be a bad idea, the problem was that the questionable organization might be the only thing some homeless people had going for them. It would be all they had until something else could take its place. I didn't want to be the one that ended up hurting my homeless brothers and sisters rather than helping. It was a complex problem, to say the least. The plan I devised would have to make the whole lot of homeless providers rethink their positions on how they treated the poor and homeless. At the same time, my plan would have to make them aware that the public would be watching their every move. Maybe that would scare them into doing what was right.

Now all I had left to do was figure out how to make my goals happen. Another problem I would have to contend with was making sure what I did didn't have a negative impact on anyone that I had known or had been friends with. That included Ken, Cass, the homeless center, the homeless, and others. In other words, when the system tried to retaliate, and I knew they would, I wanted them to just blame one person for their problems. That person was me.

The morning arrived when I was going to put my plan into action. I started calling the various media outlets to spread the word that one of the homeless, or should I say ex-homeless person, Richard Tripp, would be picketing Kansas City's biggest homeless shelter at noon.

Of course, they all wanted to know why, so I let some of the reasons out. A few of them asked, "Aren't you the homeless guy that feeds the homeless at Christmas?"

"Yes," I replied.

The majority of the newspapers and television stations were there when I pulled up at noon and started picketing the shelter. I had picked that day, that time, and that shelter for several reasons: it was the biggest; at the time it was the worst; the Kansas City Homeless Coalition was having their monthly meeting there that day; and I knew the reporters would be all over the coalition members, asking what they thought about the guy walking the picket and what they had to say about his claims that the homeless were being mistreated.

The Kansas City Homeless Coalition is a group of 501(c)(3) not-for-profit organizations that meet monthly to figure out, from their point of view, what the homeless need. My plan had been simple and to the point. I had acted in a way that no one else in the Midwest had thought to act. I knew my actions would open a lot of eyes and cause a lot of people to stand up, take notice, and start asking questions. A lot of organizations were going to have to clean up their acts. On that day, I had planted a seed in their minds. They were now fearful that one man could make a difference in the way they operated with regards to the welfare of the poor and homeless. I might add that in the public's mind, I believe I instilled my presence. Anytime people talked about homelessness in Kansas City, the name Richard Tripp would also be mentioned.

That night, when I was done picketing, I went back to my hotel room I rented that night and watched the news on several different television stations. The news about the picketing of a shelter had made every broadcast.

I hear that that particular shelter lost a lot of donations that year. They also had to cancel one of their fund-raisers, which cost them dearly. I hear the loss was to the tune of about $50,000 or so. All of the 501(c)(3)s that were associated with the homeless programs were in a panic because they thought Richard Tripp might show up at their door and picket. Because of this, they began treating their clients with respect. I really think these changes had something to do with my efforts. They were scared, and they didn't know when or if I might strike at their shelter or organization. I heard that there were all kinds of meetings to discuss me and what I might do next. As a matter of fact, a few weeks later I was driving my cab when I picked up a gentleman who worked for a health organization. **He told me he was going to work for a meeting** and he couldn't be late. Could I get him there fast?

"Sure," I said, "What's so important about the meeting?"

"Well, there's this homeless guy that we're afraid might show up and find out we're doing something wrong in our funding or something."

I said, "That's tough. What's the guy's name?"

"Richard Tripp," he said.

At that moment I knew I'd made my desired impact on the system.

Some Kind of Cop

I was staying at a different motel each night, working in my taxi until I got tired and then renting a room. Ever since I'd picketed that shelter, I kept a pretty low profile. I would work downtown, the airport, and once or twice a week I would stop by the homeless center to see Ken, find out the gossip, and pick up my mail and messages. Ken still let me use the homeless center to get my mail, and he saved telephone messages that came in for me. I wasn't planning any new attacks or activities. I thought I would let them all sweat a little before I hit them again, and I only planned to hit them again if I had to. At the time, I didn't feel I really needed to work to make my presence felt. The gossip I heard from the homeless and Ken indicated to me that the 501(c)(3) organizations were already seeing me under every bush and in every door, so to speak.

One day I stopped at the center, and Ken said, "Mr. Tripp, you got a phone message yesterday from the Homeless Coalition. They would like you to attend their next monthly meeting."

"You got to be kidding," I said.

"Nope."

"Why would they want me to come to one of their meetings?"

"I don't know, Mr. Tripp. You know you caused a lot of trouble for them. Maybe they want to be friends."

"Interesting, but I think I'll pass … On second thought, where's the meeting?"

"Well, I'm not sure where it is this month, but I can check and let you know the next time you come in," Ken said.

"Okay, Ken, you find out and let them know I'll try to make it."

Each month the coalition would move its meeting to the home base of a different member of their coalition.

The next time I stopped in at the homeless center, Ken told me that the coalition would be having its monthly meeting on Eighth Street at a Women's Family

Shelter. He said that he'd already informed the coalition that I would try to attend.

I had heard a lot about this shelter from a host of homeless women. According to them, you hated men worse when you exited the shelter than when you'd entered. Naturally, there was a reason for that. There had been a lot of rumors about the shelter's female director. But you know how rumors can be.

I went to the meeting and was greeted by a preacher who had once been the director of Metropolitan Lutheran Ministries. He was someone I'd once considered a friend, but I soon found out that that was no longer the case. I was led into a room that was divided by a curtain. As I stood shielded on one side of the curtain, I overheard a conversation between two shelter directors who were sitting on the other side of the curtain.

I heard one of them say, "I hear that Tripp is supposed to show up to the meeting today."

The other guy said. "I heard that too. I wonder who in the hell he thinks he is. Does he think he's some kind of cop or something?"

They didn't know I was on the other side of the curtain. One of the coalition members approached me and said, "Mr. Tripp, the meeting is in the other room."

I walked around the curtain and glanced over at the two shelter directors I'd heard talking. They looked surprised to see me, and I bet they were wondering if I had heard their conversation. I just smiled at them and said, "It's a nice sunny day, isn't it, gentleman?" They didn't respond.

About that time a woman, the shelter director, said, "Everybody gather around the table; it's time for the meeting to start." From the looks I was receiving, I got the impression that a lot of the people at that meeting would have liked to have slit my throat, but I just sat there and acted as if I didn't have a care in the world.

During the meeting, the coalition introduced the development of a new committee to work on homelessness. The chairperson, which was also the director of the women's shelter we were having the meeting at, asked me if I would like to be a member of this committee.

I said, "I don't see why not."

"Those in favor of adding Mr. Tripp to the committee, raise your hand."

Three or four members of the coalition raised their hand from an audience of about thirty people and I was told that I was on the committee. Three others from different 501(c)(3)s were named to the same committee. It didn't take me long to figure out that the only reason they'd nominated me for that position was to pacify me.

The meeting lasted about an hour. On the way out, I spoke to the preacher who'd been the director of Metropolitan Lutheran Ministries and asked him about the director of the women's shelter. She had worked for him before being promoted to the position she had now, and she'd also worked at other 501(c)(3) organizations. I asked him about the rumors.

"What rumors, Tripp?"

"Well, I've heard that she leads an alternative lifestyle."

"If she does, that's her business," he said.

"You're right, sir. You're right unless the other rumors are true. I've heard many times that she uses her lifestyle against the clients of that facility. That rumor has been going around the street for quite some time."

"I haven't heard the rumor, Tripp."

"Okay, Bob, I just wanted you to know the rumor, and I was interested in your opinion on the matter. Personally, I don't care what her lifestyle is, as long as she doesn't try to use it on her homeless clients. I have lots of friends that live that lifestyle."

With that, he turned on me.

"If you say anything about her to the newspapers, I'll close the homeless center," he said.

Yep, it was a threat, and it was one I couldn't really push past. There was an off chance that he might still have enough clout with Metropolitan Lutheran Ministries to pull his threat off. That's the one time I had to back down from implementing one of my plans. I didn't back down because I was afraid of him. I backed down because I felt the homeless center was needed by the homeless community.

I was still glad I went to the meeting that day. Thanks to those two shelter operators talking about me, I now had a name for my organization. It had come to me when one of them said, "I wonder who in the hell he thinks he is. Does he think he's some kind of cop or something?" I remember thinking, "God, how can I use what they just said to my advantage?" And then that little voice inside my head said, "Well, what do you want to do? You want to take care of poor people. Wait a minute, Care of Poor People—COPP." Needless to say, none of the coalition members ever again talked about me when I was within earshot.

For the next couple weeks, I tried to get a hold of the others on the committee they had nominated me for, but no one would return my calls. When I went to the next meeting, it was revealed that the chairperson had made a mistake. I couldn't be on the committee because I didn't have a 501(c)(3) classification. As a matter of fact, they revealed that I shouldn't even be attending their meetings. Needless to say, the chairperson of the coalition was the director of that shelter on Eighth Street.

I left that day with a couple of new goals. One was to obtain a 501(c)(3) certification. I cannot share my other goal at this time, but feel assured that one day I will.

Learning the Ropes

I had been organizing the Christmas Breakfast for the Homeless event for a few years before I started really considering getting a 501(c)(3) classification. It's not that I hadn't wanted the classification, it was just that I knew it would cost a lot of money to get it, and there wasn't money to spare. In fact, I was already using my own money to finance many of our events. Aside from being short on money, I didn't really have the knowledge needed to complete the required paperwork and secure the certification.

I had been invited to speak at the Unity Church of Overland Park that year. My topic of discussion was the Christmas Breakfast for the Homeless event we were having on Christmas morning down at the homeless center. I gave my presentation one Sunday. The very next day I pulled out of Sanderson's Restaurant and was driving my taxi down Main Street, when a car came up behind me and the driver started honking her horn. I kept driving down the street, and the car behind me kept honking. I looked in my rearview mirror and saw a black woman signaling for me to pull over. I did so, got out of my car, and headed back to see what she wanted. I had no idea what was on her mind.

When I reached her car, she rolled down her window and said, "My name is Tina. You're Richard Tripp, aren't you?"

"Yes, I am. Is there a problem?" I asked.

"No, Mr. Tripp. I saw you speak at Unity yesterday. I was just lucky enough to see you get in your car back there at Sanderson's. I thought I'd try to speak to you about the work you do and see if there is anything I can do to help. I'm interested in helping you with your mission to help the homeless. Have you got time for a cup of coffee or something?"

"Well, Tina, I guess I do. Let's go back to Sanderson's."

I got back in my car, and she followed me to the restaurant. We went inside, got some coffee, and started talking. During the course of our conversation, Tina mentioned that she had done work with a lot of the not-for-profits in the city. I mentioned to her that I had wanted to go that direction with my group, but I didn't know how to set it up.

She said, "Well, I have a friend who could probably help you get everything in order. It probably wouldn't cost much to get your 501. I could give him a call, set up a meeting, and we can see what he says."

"Okay, do that and let me know. I can be reached at the homeless center."

"Okay, Mr. Tripp, I'll be in touch."

As we left the restaurant, I thanked her for any help she might be able to provide. Then I went back to work. A few days later, I stopped by the homeless center. Ken told me that I had received a message from a woman who wanted me to return her call. She had left her number, so I used Ken's phone to call her.

The voice on the other end of the line said, "Mr. Tripp, this is Tina, the woman you spoke to the other day at Sanderson's. I spoke to Mr. Bird, the gentleman I told you about. He's the one who helps set up 501s, and he would like me to set up a meeting with you."

"Okay, Tina, can you make the meeting for ten o'clock Friday morning here at the homeless center? It's located at Ninth and Magee."

"That sounds good. We'll be there, Mr. Tripp."

I spent the rest of my week working as usual, but I must admit that Friday's meeting was on my mind a lot. Getting that 501(c)(3) classification would make a lot of difference in how we could operate. Up until now we hadn't been able to give receipts to people for any of the materials they donated. I was willing to bet that if COPP were a 501(c)(3), people would donate a lot more because they'd be getting a tax write-off. Considering that prospect alone was enough to keep the meeting on my mind.

Friday rolled around and Tina walked into the homeless center with Mr. Bird. We got right down to business. The gentleman seemed like he knew what he was doing. He was able to explain a few things to me about setting up boards, and he gave me advice about what kinds of people I should get to sit on my board. Needless to say, I dropped my guard. He was very convincing when he told me how he really wanted to help me get COPP up and running. He told me he could get everything set up for five hundred dollars. I knew that was a good price. I told him I didn't have the money, but I could probably get it by the next week. He said that was fine and that he would start getting the paperwork in order. For the next week, I worked my taxi day and night, trying to make the five hundred dollars I needed to give to Mr. Bird. And like a dummy, one week later I handed him the money.

A few days later, Mr. Bird called me and said that he had the paperwork done, but in order to get everything filed, he would need another one thousand dollars so his lawyer could set everything up. I was furious, and I let him know it. "What in the hell, you mean another thousand dollars? You said we could get this whole thing done for five hundred dollars."

He said, "No, Mr. Tripp, you misunderstood me. I said the five hundred dollars was my consulting fee."

"Well, Mr. Bird, you're lucky we're talking on the phone, because if I could get my hands on you right now, I would take five hundred dollars out of your ass."

He hung up the phone, and that was the last time I ever heard from Mr. Bird. Come to think of it, I haven't heard his name anywhere since. I guess he left town.

A few days later, Tina came into the homeless center and told me that she'd had no idea that Mr. Bird was a con artist. She said she'd met him through a mutual friend. At any rate, she apologized for introducing us. I asked her if she had an address for the man. She gave me the one she had, but there was no such place.

I'm not usually that stupid with my money, but we all get taken once in a while. I guess it had been my turn. I had wanted that 501(c)(3) so bad that I let common sense walk out the door.

After all, the guy had put on a performance as good as any actor I'd ever seen, and although I was out the five hundred dollars, he had given me some good tips on putting the board together. So I started doing that. My first board members were homeless people. It sounds silly, but at the time it seemed like the right thing to do. When I put together that first board, I took anybody who was willing to serve. It isn't like that today. I've learned that you need good, upstanding, civic/business-oriented people sitting on your board. Don't get me wrong, I'm not saying you shouldn't have those who are in need on your board, but when you're dealing with a not-for-profit, it makes better sense to have board members who are known in your community for certain jobs rather than board members who are not.

Just because I had lost that five hundred dollars to a con artist didn't mean I was going to give up. If nothing else, it made me more determined to succeed. The classification was just going to have to wait a while longer. At that time, I was speaking to a lot of churches and clubs, and I often shared my dream of setting up a 501(c)(3). Following a speaking gig at a men's group, one of the attendees approached me. He told me that he was a lawyer, and he said he would help me file the paperwork to secure the tax-exempt classification. The best part was that he volunteered to do the work for free. About six months later COPP was granted its 501(c)(3) classification.

Building Bridges

When I started COPP, I was aware of some of the problems I would have getting different denominations to see things my way. I had to come up with a way of appealing to the masses of different congregations. In Kansas City, there is a program on the radio every Sunday morning called *Religion on the Line.* It's the top-rated show in its time slot. The announcers back when I started COPP were three clergy members from three different denominations.

One was a minister from Community Christian Church in Kansas City. His name was Pastor Robert Hill. The second was Father Tom Savage from the Catholic Church, and the third was a rabbi named Michael Zedec. He was the head rabbi at the biggest Jewish synagogue in Kansas City. At the time, I didn't know any of these gentlemen, but I felt I needed to meet them if I was going to make a difference in Kansas City's religious community and influence the masses to help me. In a sense, one might say that I stalked them.

I listened to their radio program for more than a month. One day I heard that all three men would be making an appearance together at a Lutheran church in Kansas City. I went to the church and listened as they gave their speeches. What I heard was impressive. When the speeches were over, I introduced myself to each of the men. I also handed each man a flyer about an upcoming COPP event I was planning. It was a short introduction, but I felt I'd gotten my foot in the door.

After a week or so had passed, I made the first of what would eventually be many appointments to speak to these gentlemen. The first clergyman I approached was Pastor Hill of Community Christian Church. We had a very good meeting, and he told me that he and his congregation would help COPP's effort in any way they could. He also said he would speak to Father Savage and Rabbi Zedec about my events.

The second clergyman I approached was Father Savage. He was intrigued by how I ran COPP events. He, too, agreed to talk to his congregation about the organization.

I found that the third gentleman, Rabbi Zedec, scared me the most. With him I was stepping outside my comfort zone. I didn't know the first thing about the Jewish religion, and I was afraid I might say something to get tossed out on my ear, but that never happen. Instead, we became good friends. I believe this happened because he knew I was sincere in my mission to help those in need. I will have you know that Rabbi Zedec is one very smart man. He's also someone I respect very much. He earns this respect by heading straight to the point on any matter he is faced with.

I remember the day I walked into his office, told him my story, explained to him my plan, and spelled out the reasons why I wanted to get involved. He stared at me as if he was looking right into my soul. It's a weird feeling to feel as if you're in the presence of someone who is that close to God, but that's how he made me feel—then and now—and I'm not even Jewish. Following that meeting in his office, he followed me out the door of the synagogue. I think he wanted to see if I was for real; I think he was checking to see if I was driving a taxi like my story said I was.

Over the next several months, those gentlemen began to talk about me on their radio show, and we continued to meet from time to time. Then something happened that I will never forget. Rabbi Zedec called me one day and asked me if I would like to speak to his congregation at their Friday night Shabbat. He wanted me to tell his congregation about COPP and its events. I agreed, but my stomach was in knots for the rest of that week. The closer Friday night got, the more scared I got, but I was determined to speak. In hindsight, I think I was so nervous because I didn't yet know just how loving and compassionate our Jewish brothers and sisters are. I am so glad I didn't back out of that speaking engagement. I have never met a more loving and compassionate people.

I met several people that night who have helped me and stood by me ever since. If need be, I would give my life for these friends. I care very much for both my Christian family of brothers and sisters and my Jewish family of brothers and sisters. It is written in most religious books to love thy brothers and sisters as thyself. The Bible, Torah, Koran, and even the Egyptian book of the dead have such scriptures. That being said, a couple of very special Jewish brothers and sisters have helped me immensely over the years. They're on the COPP board, and without them many members of Kansas City's poor and homeless population may have perished. I'm not going to single them out, but they know who they are, and I'm also quite sure they know how I feel about them.

At times I have been criticized for the way I operate COPP, but I have held fast to my ideals. I believe an entire community should be involved in helping other community members, regardless of race, creed, color, or sexual orientation. We're all brothers and sisters, regardless of our political and individual differences. It is a soul-lifting experience for me to watch an entire community work together to help the poor and homeless at COPP events. Watching the Holy Spirit work between the different races and faiths toward a common goal—showing those who are down and out that God hasn't forgotten them—provides a high like no other.

The truth is that when you or your children are hurting, you don't much care who helps you. You don't stop to consider the do-gooder's race, faith, or political views. You just thank God that somebody cares enough to help at all. I love watching Jews, gentiles, and members of other faiths as they mingle at COPP events and work together toward a common goal—showing the poor and homeless that someone cares.

I have learned that every religious book in the world tells its readers how they should be treating our poor and homeless brothers and sisters. The Bible, the Torah, the Koran, and even the Egyptian Book of the Dead teach the importance of compassion. It is an eye-opening experience to watch a multitude of faiths work together to spread the love of a supreme being.

From time to time I have been criticized by my own Christian brothers and sisters because I am willing to speak to the congregation of any denomination's church and because I am willing to accept funds from any denomination in order to do my work. I refer my critics back to the notion that you don't care who helps you when you're hurting. You don't take time to question political views and sexual orientations when you're in need and a helping hand is being extended. In the same regard, I don't care who supports COPP and its events, as long as we are able to get the job done and save lives. I'm reminded of Jesus and the Samaritan woman who gave him a glass of water. It's a story about helping others, regardless of religion or political views.

With all that having been said, another lesson I have learned is that COPP cannot rely on a single denomination or faith to carry it along. I have seen a lot of good programs go out the door because they relied too heavily on a single source of income from one denomination or religious sect. If your program has only one benefactor, it can quickly lose its funding if it refuses to act as a puppet for the moneyman. This is not the case with COPP. We rely on multiple sources of income from all faiths and denominations. This prevents COPP from shying away from the path or the programs it wants to pursue. I try very hard not to let anything or anyone dictate our progress.

While I had connected with a lot of the religious community by getting involved with *Religion on the Line* and befriending those three prominent members of the clergy, the simple fact was, it wasn't enough. When COPP began to organize its events, my idea was to bring the whole community together to help those who were down and out, as opposed to turning to a single faction of the community for aid. I hadn't meant to single out religious groups. I needed to come up with a plan to get the rest of the community involved. My first experience working with the radio had gone well, so I opted to start there. I decided that I would give as many interviews as I could, with as many radio stations as would have me. My interviews were aired on stations with a variety of formats—talk, hard rock, country, easy listening. Wherever I could get my foot in the door, I gave an interview.

The problem was that my message wasn't getting out. There were only so many time slots dedicated to community affairs on the radio stations in my community. Those time slots were usually slated for either early morning or late at night, when most people are asleep, or they were available on the weekend. I didn't have an advertising budget like most not-for-profits, and I was having a hard time promoting COPP events and COPP itself as an organization. I decided that I needed to find a couple of radio stations that I felt really cared about the community. I needed their help pushing my agenda.

You might say I finally got lucky when I approached 61 Country, one of Kansas City's country stations. In those days, back when I had just begun holding the Christmas Breakfast for the Homeless, their programming director was a gentleman named Ted Cramer. He made the decision to give me a thirty-second public service announcement, which the station played numerous times the week of Christmas to help me get donations for the homeless. That week, his station also donated one hundred pairs of long john underwear to give out to the homeless. I must have heard that PSA a hundred times that week. It really brought in the donations, and we had a great event. At the same time, that PSA got my name and the organization's name out to the public more than any other method had to date. That PSA was played at all hours of the day and night, and many people heard about us.

Because I'd had so much success in my dealings with 61 Country, an AM station, the idea hit me that maybe now it was time I should approach an FM radio station. In hindsight, I believe this was one of the best decisions I ever made in my life. Aside from getting the word out about COPP, I met a group of professionals that really seemed to care about their community.

My relationship with Country 94.1 KFKF started when I sent an e-mail to Randy Birch, the station's news director. He invited me to come down to the station and record a thirty-minute public service program. I was a little apprehensive about having a full thirty minutes to tell the public what COPP was about and how they could help, but I agreed. I couldn't turn the opportunity down. I showed up at the station, not really knowing what to expect. I just knew that I had to say the right things in order to persuade the public to get involved with COPP.

As I waited in the reception area with thoughts running through my mind, Randy Birch walked up to me and said, "Richard Tripp?"

I responded, "Yes, sir."

"I'm Randy Birch, News Director here at KFKF. Are you ready to go do the show?"

"I guess," I replied.

I think he could see that I was a little apprehensive. He said, "Don't worry, Mr. Tripp. We'll have some fun with it. Can I get you a cup of coffee or a soft drink?"

"No, thank you," I replied.

"Okay, then let's head into the studio and get started."

I followed him through a door, then down and around a hallway to the studio. The little room was just big enough to accommodate Randy's seat in front of the control panel and two other chairs, which were situated in front of a couple of microphones.

He started the show by saying, "Ladies and gentlemen, have we got a show for you today. Richard Tripp, the director of Care of Poor People, is here to tell us about his organization and how you can help Kansas City's poor and homeless."

That is how the relationship between COPP and KFKF started. After we'd recorded that first show, Randy took me around the rest of the station and introduced me to everyone on the KFKF staff. I became good friends with these people over the years. They eventually felt more like family than friends. During the taping of one of my radio shows, I met *Morning Country Club Show* producer Jim Daniels, station manager Dale Carter, and his partner on the *Morning Country Club Show*, Mary McKenna. Someone made the comment, "I wish there was more we could do to help you, Richard."

"Well, since you brought it up, why not hold a radio-thon for COPP?" I replied.

They all looked at each other a bit dumbfounded. I don't think it was something they'd expected me to say. Jim spoke up and said, "What kind of radiothon?"

"Well, maybe you could get people to bring me used and new clothing to help the homeless."

"I tell you what, Richard, let me talk to our marketing department and see what they think," Jim said.

"Okay, Jim. Give me a call and let me know."

The rest is history. Every November KFKF sets aside a day for the Care of Poor People Radio-thon where we collect at least a semi trailer truckload of warm clothes to be handed out at COPP survival events. We collect clothing for men, women, and children; hygiene items; and cash donations. Not only does KFKF hold the radio-thon for COPP, but the majority of the station's DJs attend the survival event each year to watch as the donations are given out to the poor. As I have said, over the years I've learned to use the media to my advantage. When you're able to gather that much media involvement, eventually the people listening to the stations you're on start coming out to help.

Doing My Own Thing

When I was released from the hospital in 1995, just weeks prior to my first encounter with Mark Victor Hansen, I had already been holding the Christmas Breakfast for the Homeless event in Kansas City for a couple of years. At the time, it was the only event I organized each year. But once I came under Mark's influence and secured some financial backing from some of his friends at local churches, like Unity Church of Overland Park, we started an additional event on Thanksgiving weekend. There was no doubt that the Christmas Breakfast for the Homeless had answered a need. Now there was a new need. Many of the poor and homeless needed warm clothing *before* Christmas. Not having the materials needed to survive on the streets during cold weather conditions had led to the discovery of more than one homeless person's body. Because of this, I decided to organize two events each year. That number grew to three after 1995.

Organizing three events each year was the norm until the shelters finally decided that COPP was making them look bad on Christmas morning. In 1996 the shelters reversed their policies and decided to allow the homeless to remain indoors on Christmas morning. I think they thought that would put a stop to Richard Tripp and COPP. Their assumption was just another underestimation of my abilities by the powers that be. All it did was free me up to address a poor and homeless need that was falling through the cracks—the need for summer-type clothing.

It took eight years of Christmas Breakfast for the Homeless before the other 501s became wise enough to host their own events instead of kicking the poor and homeless out on Christmas morning. During those years, I had formed COPP, put together a board, and received 501(c)(3) certification. It had been a long, hard battle, but I had succeeded in making it happen. I had, and still have, a vision for the future. Every time something gets in my way, instead of running from it, I figure out a way to use the adversity to my advantage. I did this with common street sense and God's help.

As I mentioned previously, I got to where I am today by playing the part of a dumb cab driver. Not having a college degree or even a high school diploma does not mean that I am unintelligent when it comes to dealing with the public and understanding the problems of the poor and homeless. Using the media to make a difference for those who are hurting wasn't a dumb move either.

When I was a kid, my father used to talk about me to other people. He'd say, "Is my kid crazy? Yep, crazy like a fox." The truth is that, though I often play dumb, it's usually an act. I try to develop a game plan before I make a move. I like to know what I'm facing, know the different actions my opponents might take, and know there's a backup plan in the wings if things start to go wrong. Of course, nobody is buying the dumb, crazy cab driver routine anymore, but it did work for quite a few years.

When I started COPP, I knew I would have to operate different than the other groups. I couldn't count on securing funding in the same ways they did. You might say I was independent. I chose to take this route because I didn't want my organization to be like any other. When I started COPP, I focused on two objectives: where do I get funding, and how do I make COPP the first organization people think of when they think about helping the poor.

The first part was easy. I was a cab driver. I could solicit the people I was picking up at the airport for contributions to keep the organization from going under. I never knew what big shot I might have just picked up. What I did know was that I had thirty minutes to try to get them to make a donation and to convince them that they should help me spread the word about COPP. It was often a hard sell, but I knew word would eventually get around if I told my story to enough people. If I hooked just one person out of every one hundred, it was worth it.

COPP was famous around the country before the donor networks in Kansas City were aware of what I had been up to. The majority of COPP's funding was coming in from across the country, not from local donors, as was the case with most local organizations.

Distinguishing COPP from similar organizations and making COPP people's preferred choice was going to require some effort. After noticing that all the shelters mimicked each other's events and held them at basically the same time, COPP made a conscious effort to shake it up. The organization purposely avoided holding events on days when the other 501s were holding events. When it came time to publicize an event, COPP was usually the only organization in the running for coverage. We'd purposely scheduled our event on a day when no one else was having one. Eliminating the competition for media attention made it easy to get newspaper, radio, and television coverage. At its inception, this was a novel idea.

The same was true of the annual survival event At both the survival event, and the spring break event, we provide the materials the poor and homeless need to survive on the streets, alleys, and bridges across America, along with lots of other services, including Kansas City's biggest pot luck dinner.

At the survival events we provide winter materials, and the spring break events we provide summer type clothing and other materials. The survival event is always held the Saturday after Thanksgiving.

"Why?" you ask.

We chose this date because there was nothing else going on. These were slow news days. COPP's annual survival event would cover the pages of Sunday's paper. The same was true of Spring Break for the Homeless. It was always held on the Saturday before Easter.

"Why?" you ask.

This strategic scheduling almost guaranteed that COPP would have coverage in Easter Sunday's paper. Small ideas like these helped COPP flourish over the past fourteen years or so. Of course, meeting Mark Victor Hansen didn't hurt. COPP received major publicity with the publishing of Hansen's book *Chicken Soup for the Soul.*

I might add that I have come up with more ideas for the future. I want to take COPP to the frontlines of the war on poverty. I want to make a difference in the lives of those who are hurting, doing the impossible, and still making it look good. I do not want to restrict this fight to Kansas City; I want to take it around the world. We are on our way.

Spring Break for the Homeless

Several ministers from different denominations expressed an interest in supporting COPP via both finances and materials. These churches also said that they would like to see additional events added to the COPP calendar. With supplies and donations promised, I decided that COPP was going to do something that had never been done before.

I called my new idea Spring Break for the Homeless. That first year in 1996, my timing wasn't the best. I decided to hold the event on Good Friday. This proved to be a bad idea. But you learn with trial and error. The problem was I didn't have a building. What I decided to do was hold the event outside at the homeless center. The homeless center at that time was too little to hold the hundreds of people we expected to show up for the event

All the businesses on the block, except for the homeless center, were closed for Good Friday. That meant COPP had use of the entire block for its event. All I had to do was get a block party permit from the city so we could block off the street. And although the permit was going to cost fifty dollars, I had a donor who was willing to foot the bill. I jumped through all the hoops the city makes you go through to get the permit, and we were on our way to another successful event.

As always, I let the word out to both the public and the homeless that COPP was going be holding an event outside the homeless center on Good Friday. After a story ran in the *Kansas City Star* newspaper, material and monetary donations started coming in. The day before the event, I was confident that everything would go pretty smooth. We had everything I thought we would need: grills, tables, chairs, and portable toilets being delivered the next day. And the best thing was, thanks to COPP' supporters, everything was paid for.

The next morning, I arrived at the homeless center at about nine o'clock. Shortly after, the rental equipment started showing up, and my team of volunteers had arrived to begin setting up. My mother had come to witness me in action. Upon her arrival I said, "Mom, let's go across the street and get a cup of coffee over at Tom's."

We'd been in the café for about ten minutes when one of the homeless men who was helping set up rushed in and said, "Tripp, you better get over to the homeless center. Ken wants you."

"Why? What does he want?"

"I don't know. He said something about the city shutting down the event."

"What?" I exclaimed. "Mom, I'll be right back."

I rushed over to the center, found Ken, and immediately asked, "What's going on?"

He said, "Mr. Tripp, I took down this number for you. It's someone at City Hall. This person claims you can't have the event."

"Give me the number. I'll give them a call and find out what they're talking about, Ken. I have the damn permit right here."

"Well, here's the number and the extension of the guy you're supposed to talk to."

I dialed the number, and a man picked up on the other end.

"This is Richard Tripp. I hear you called over to the homeless center to speak to me."

"Well, yes I did, Mr. Tripp. It seems we made a little mistake in giving you that block party permit. You can't hold your event."

"What in the hell do you mean? I have the permit right here in my hand, and rental equipment is arriving as we speak. I've spent a thousand dollars putting this event together."

"Well, be that as it may, you still can't block the street off and have the event."

About that time my mother walked in and said, "What's going on, Rick?"

I put my hand over the phone and asked, "What should I do, Mom?"

"Well, Son, I can only tell you what I would do."

"What's that?"

"If it was me, I'd tell them to stick it in their ear, and I'd have the event anyway. It's really too late for you to make changes, you know."

I thought about it for a minute and said, "Sir, it's too late for me to change the event. I'm going to go ahead with it."

There was a pause on the other end of the line before the guy said, "Then I'll send the police on over."

By that time I was really pissed.

I said, "You can send the whole department, but I'm still going have my event," and with that I hung up.

I knew I was probably in some deep trouble, but I had decided that the only way they were going to stop me from having the event was to put me in jail. I suspected that the sudden permit reversal was politically motivated. The shelters were still trying to make me look bad, and they'd almost succeeded. Think of how bad it would look to my donors if I took their donations and never held the event. That thought was running through my head as I hung up the phone.

I immediately began calling TV newsrooms. Each station I talked to said they would send a news crew out. The news crews and the police showed up at about the same time. The cameras were rolling when I showed the police my permit. We exchanged a few words about the situation, and it was finally decided that City Hall was in the wrong. The permit had been issued, and the event would go on.

The event was a success, and the day was a turning point in my life. I proved that the old adage, "You can't fight City Hall," isn't always true. Had I backed down and let them cancel the event, who knows where I'd be today. Even today, COPP's bouts with City Hall continue. But every year for the past fourteen years, City Hall has given COPP its own day in a Proclamation of Care of Poor People Day, which is signed by the mayor and the members of the city council. I might add that Spring Break for the Homeless is now a nationwide event that's always held the Saturday before Easter. Millions of homeless people are helped that day. When I think about the first Spring Break for the Homeless, I'm always amazed that we pulled it off. Then again, I am sure God had his hands all over it, and if you have him with you, who can stand against you?

Most Underestimate How Far I Will Go to Make a Difference

While I haven't been to the top of the mountain and seen what's on the other side, like one of my idols, Martin Luther King Jr., I still have my own dream. Better yet, I have a destiny; that destiny is to leave this world in better shape than when I came into it. My destiny is to show those who think no one cares, that even though they might be down our heavenly father hasn't forgotten them in their time of need. He has placed it on my heart, and the hearts of others, to make a change for those hurting, regardless of the consequences to ourselves. We know we are to forge forward, showing his love and his strength to the downtrodden, and we are to go up against the system without fear. It matters not to me if I'm fighting against the shelters or the dangers on streets. God has given me the tools to wage war on both fronts. I've been called the devil, and I have been called a saint. Neither is true. Some even call me a legend. It's never really bothered or affected me to hear what others think of me.

I've explained many of the battles I've fought against the shelters. I will now share some of the problems I've encountered at COPP events and on the streets.

To most, I am known as a person who cares about people. To a few, my caring personality has at times been mistaken for weakness. Those people soon learn that caring and trying to make a difference in the lives of the poor does not make me a pushover. For instance, I learned from the childless adults who wanted toys at that first Christmas event that there will always be someone out there trying to figure out a way to use your good deeds to their advantage. After the second Christmas breakfast, I was in my cab at the Greyhound Bus Station when several street hustlers approached me and tried to sell me long john underwear. This was same underwear I had just given out to the poor. Come to find out, the hustlers had bought the underwear from some of the poor people who'd attended the breakfast. They had given them a couple of dollars for it and were trying to sell it for five dollars a pair. I was furious, but what could I do. The next year I made it harder for the hustlers. Before handing the underwear out to the homeless, we took everything out of the original packaging. It might have not completely stopped the hustlers, but I bet it put a big damper on their plans.

Throughout the years I've learned many things. In some cases, I not only need to put the materials into people's hands, I also need to make an effort to be sure the materials are being used appropriately. I've also learned that there will always be someone who thinks they can profit from my hard work.

One Christmas, COPP collected a great supply of new toys that we were going to give out to the homeless kids. The news got out, and an additional fifteen to twenty women who'd never been to one of our events showed up for the handout. They were just there for the toys. The problem was that they didn't have any kids with them. Something just wasn't right about the situation.

A few of the women were accompanied by men in gold chains who weren't dressed like they were poor or homeless, and I was sure I'd seen several of the women on the street corners. It didn't take me long to figure out what was up. The problem was that I had to figure out what to do about it.

I was thinking about the situation when a homeless woman approached me with her kids and said, "Hey Tripp, you know who those guys are?"

"No. Why?"

"Hey, man, they're here to get all the good toys to sell. None of them women got kids. They're streetwalkers."

"Don't worry about it. I'll take care of it," I told her.

I told my staff to take the expensive toys into the other room, where Santa would hand them out to the children. The cheaper toys would be left under the tree for those who didn't have kids with them. When it came time to distribute the gifts that morning, I had everybody form two lines—one line for adults with children and the other for adults without children. Naturally, there was some flack. The pimps who thought they were going to turn this charitable event into their own personal payday were the most upset. Enough of my staff was with me that we didn't have any physically motivated outbursts. That was the last time the pimps tried to crash one of my events.

Even with thousands in attendance, most COPP events generate zero problems. To tell you the truth, when a problem does arise, the homeless usually police themselves before things get out of hand. I have on occasion talked a troublemaker or two into leaving an event. On rare occasions, I might have to break up a fight. I have a reputation among the homeless as being someone who's not afraid to get physical. I always try to talk to a troublemaker before allowing a situation to become physical. I might add that one of my guests or myself must be threatened before a situation accelerates to a physical confrontation. Using force is a last resort. And I'm proud to report that not one of our volunteers has ever been threatened during a COPP event.

There was an instance a few years ago when we had a worker from another organization come down to help us at one of our events. A client of hers had followed her and was spreading the word that he and his little gang of street thugs were going to jump her at my event. One of the homeless brothers found me and told me what was supposed to happen. I found the gang leader and talked him into going into the restroom with me for a little talk. I told him I had some weed hidden in there. He was more than ready to go in and try some of it.

When we got into the restroom, I shut the door, locked it, and turned around.

He said, "Hey, man, where's the weed?"

I said, "I'm sorry, I lied."

"Well, why did you invite me in here?"

"Because you and I are going have a talk about you and your crew leaving my event."

His eyes got big, and I could tell I had his attention. I won't go into detail about what I told him, but he got an attitude adjustment in that restroom. It's funny how those gang leaders aren't so bad once you get them away from their crew. Anyway, we had a talk, and he decided he and his crew would leave without incident.

I don't like having to threaten the use of physical harm, but sometimes you use what works. It's important to always leave the person with an out. If I'd have tried that stunt in front of that gang leader's crew, he would have felt obligated to give me trouble, just to keep his reputation intact. By taking him into the restroom with just me, he was able to make up any excuse he wanted to explain their quick departure from my event. They left without causing trouble; that was all that really mattered to me.

There have been other times during the years when I have had to give attitude adjustments to people on the streets outside of my events. I am not fond of people who prey on the poor and homeless in my community. Don't get me wrong. I don't try to be a vigilante or anything like that. There are just certain times when you see someone being hurt and you have to put your butt on the line to stop the injustice.

For instance, I pulled up to the Greyhound Bus Station one day and saw a woman sitting outside. Her clothes were torn, and she was crying.

I got out of my taxi and walked over to her. At first, she wouldn't even look up at me. I said, "Miss, is something wrong?"

When she did look up at me, I could see she had been beaten up. I asked, "What happened to you?"

I mean, it was very apparent what had happened to her, but at the same time she wasn't talking. She just looked at me with a pitiful look on her face and kept crying.

I said, "Miss, would you like me to call the police or an ambulance for you?"

She finally spoke and said, "I don't know."

Knowing something bad had happened to her, I called the police. It was a while before they showed up, so I had her get in the backseat of my taxi while we waited. She finally broke her silence and told me what had happened to her. And the more she told me, the madder I got.

It seems she was a runaway from one of the farming communities here in Missouri. She had come into town on the bus the night before, and a couple of the street thugs that hang around the bus station had talked her into going to one of the old abandoned buildings to stay with them for the night. It's obvious that she shouldn't have gone with or trusted them, but she was just a dumb kid about 17. She'd probably never even been out of her home community. At any rate, they ended up raping her and beating her up.

As her story progressed, so did my anger. I guess I was thinking, "What if this had happened to one of my daughters?" I asked her what the men looked like, and she described them. As soon as I heard the description, I knew who she was talking about. She said that one of the men had an arm with no hand, and she explained how this man just kept hitting her with that arm. About that time, the police showed up. I told them what she had told me and where they might find the assailants. The police got an ambulance for the girl and told me that the detectives would be getting in touch with me. When the police left, I was still so outraged at what they had done to this little girl that I went looking for them. I tell you, it is good the police found those men before I did. If I'd have caught up with them first, there wouldn't have been enough left of them for the police to take to jail.

A few months later, the men were on trial. I had to go to court to explain what the girl had told me that day at the bus station. One of the reasons I had to testify was because there was a chance these clowns would get off if I didn't. The reason being, once that girl got back home to her family, she committed suicide My testimony was the only chance the prosecutor had at a conviction, and there was no way I was going to allow that trash to be put back out on the streets. I told the jury what that little girl had told me, and the men were put away for a long time. I expect that one of these years they'll get out and come looking for me.

After the trial, the girl's parents thanked me for helping their daughter. They were from a religious sect, the type you see riding in horse-drawn buggies in little towns across Missouri. Her mother told me that she was surprised her daughter had spoken to me. She had apparently taken a vow of silence before she had run away from home. I guess that's why it took so long to get the girl to speak to me about what had happened to her. I can assure you, it's a memory I try not to think about. The hurt and confusion I saw in that girl's eyes still get to me. It's insane that someone could do that much harm to another human being.

Another time, there was a homeless gentleman here in town who knew he had AIDS. He was purposely going around infecting the homeless women on the streets. It seemed that the police couldn't do anything about it, or they didn't give a damn how many people he infected. I felt compelled to have a heart-to-heart talk with the gentleman.

I tried to talk to him in a compassionate way about the problem he was causing, but he laughed at me and said, "Tripp, it isn't any of your business who I sleep with. There isn't anything you can do about it. I'm dying anyway; I'll take a few with me."

He had a point. There wasn't any sense in threatening him with death because he was already dying. I wouldn't have gone that far anyway, but he had definitely pushed my buttons when he laughed at me. I did the only thing I could think to do. I grabbed him, pushed him up against the wall like I was going hit him, and said, "There are a lot of things that are worse than death, my friend. You're right. I'm not going kill you, but I'll tell you this. If I hear that you've infected any more of the women on the street, I'll personally make sure that you'll be in pain every day for the rest of your life, and don't worry, I know how to inflict pain without killing you. Do I make myself clear?" He didn't know the threat was really a big bluff on my part. I guess he believed me, because it didn't take long for him to leave town. And I didn't hear of any more women he infected in Kansas City.

I'm not really proud of having to be a heavy at times, but I am proud of being able to make the streets less dangerous for those living on them. These stories happened in my past, and I could tell many more. Today, I'm a lot older, and, to a point, I'm wiser. I don't get physical in a situation unless it's absolutely necessary.

COPP Shops

One of the projects I intend to eventually see through is called "COPP Shops," a day-labor project for the homeless. While there are a lot of day-labor places out there, none of them really gives a hand up to the poor and homeless. My vision includes not only providing them pay-by-the-day wages, which they need to survive, but also giving them good job skills for, say, ninety days. After that, they'll be able to go to work on a permanent basis for a company we place them with, at a wage that they can actually live on. They'll be able to live their part of the American dream, not just survive in it. That is one of our future goals.

Having a vision is good, but making it work is better. We are still working out several problems associated with getting the COPP Shops started. But the key to making the program work is workman's compensation insurance. Once I figure out a way around that problem, the rest will seem easy. The problem is the high cost of the insurance. Others have tried to start programs similar to the COPP Shops, and they have run into the same problem. I know there is an answer. Maybe someone reading this book will have the answer. If so, please contact me.

Another problem we face is finding the basic start-up money it would take to make the program a success. A lot of the profits from this book will help fund this important project, and, God willing, I'll see this project up and running across America before I leave this earth. If not, I pray some other person picks up the torch and makes it happen. For I believe the old adage, "giving a person a fish is helpful for one meal, but teaching someone to fish will be good for life." In other words, the best way to take care of those who are down and out, is to teach them how to help themselves. By training them in a trade, they can support themselves for life.

Here are some examples of what I hope to accomplish with COPP Shops:

COPP Shops seeks partners to develop a Nonprofit Labor Pool.

The COPP Shops Nonprofit Labor Pool would offer an effective, competitive, fair alternative to conventional labor pools. Such a nonprofit labor pool would provide things to both labor-pool workers and their employers that conventional labor pools do not.

To labor-pool workers, the COPP Shops would offer:

- Hourly wages above the state and federal minimum wage
- Necessary tools and equipment for each job, without wage deductions
- Transportation to and from each job, without wage deductions
- Predictable, reliable jobs each day, without long, futile waits in line
- Skill assessment with counseling and referrals for education, job—and life-skill training, and permanent employment, including self-employment and micro enterprise development
- Case management and other supportive services, including shelter and housing placement and assistance; physical and mental health referrals and treatment; referrals and treatment for substance abuse; and peer-support groups for building self-confidence and independence, as well as addressing employment obstacles, problems, and issues

To employers, the COPP Shops would offer:

- Workers who are more reliable, stable, and strongly motivated
- Workers who are tested for skills and substance abuse
- Workers who are receiving case management and other supportive services and are pursuing permanent, stable employment
- Workers as and when needed, on a day-to-day basis, with the paperwork to put them to work already taken care of
- Better workers but lower labor costs to employers who let us do their job advertising, interviewing, and screening, as well as processing their payroll, including workman's compensation and insurance

COPP Shops seeks nonprofit labor-pool partners to provide these services:

- Pooling worker's compensation and insurance coverage and costs

- Substance-abuse testing, assessment, and treatment
- Physical and mental health testing, assessment, and treatment
- Literacy, life-skills, and job-skills assessment, development, and training
- Self-employment, micro enterprise, and business-skills assessment, development, and support
- Case management, with referrals and linkage to appropriate services
- Shelter, transitional housing, and supportive housing
- Transportation to and from job sites
- Collaboration in community networking and marketing

Naturally, it would take the whole community to make this happen.

While I personally believe the COPP Shops are one of the future answers to fighting poverty in America, we still have many more problems that not only the down-and-out will have to face, but also that the caregivers trying to make a difference for those hurting will have to face at the same time.

Here is a case in point. Recently, various cities across America passed laws that make it a crime to feed the poor and homeless at city parks or other places where the poor and homeless hang out. Two of those cities are Las Vegas, Nevada, and Orlando, Florida. I believe it's just a matter of time before other cities do the same. Many caregivers will likely stop their feeding programs for fear of being arrested for feeding the poor and homeless.

Increasingly vicious laws designed to push the homeless out of communities nationwide appear intent on testing the lengths they can go to expel the homeless population. Some people will do anything to avoid having to see, let alone help, the less fortunate. It seems that in the face of rising homelessness, cities across the country are increasingly trying to push desperate people out of sight and out of mind. In addition to anti-panhandling, anti-camping, and anti-loitering ordinances, some cities are targeting the few remaining public spaces where homeless people can go during the day. This includes parks and libraries right here in my community. When I was homeless back in 1990, living down by the river, it was a common practice for the railroad to burn homeless camps alongside their train tracks. They may deny the practice, but I have seen it happen personally. They got away with it because they own the right of way. When something like that happens and COPP finds out about it, we try to re-supply those hurting with the materials they need to rebuild their camps. Some would say we're providing a Band-Aid, and I'd have to agree. But to help those who are down and out, until my community leaders decide to build enough affordable housing for those that are displaced in our community, we will do what it takes to help them survive, Band-Aid or not.

As far as the Kansas City libraries are concerned, it is bad for the homeless here, but our city fathers haven't yet come up with a program like they have in San Francisco. There they have a program called Homeward Bound. The purpose of the program is to give the homeless a one-way ticket out of town so people don't complain about the homeless who gather at their library during the day. According to news sources, I have heard that they hand out over one thousand tickets a year to the homeless of that city. The fact of the matter is that the library is about the only place the homeless can turn to get out of the heat or cold during the day. With more cities passing code-of-conduct policies that allow library staff to banish people from the library, it is really getting to be a catch-22 for the homeless. A recent article I saw about the library in Richmond, Virginia, tells how the city enacted new codes of conduct allowing library staff to banish people who bring in more than two book bags, bags over eighteen inches in length, plastic bags, bed rolls, or luggage. People whose personal hygiene is so offensive as to constitute a nuisance to other people, or those that change clothes in the bathroom, can also be removed from the library. The revised codes further state that failure to comply with the library rules may result in arrest.

I personally believe that the rise in homelessness is feeding the rise in city ordinances and policies that target the homeless. Not only are these things happening in libraries around our nation, but also right here in my own community. It's just a matter of time before Kansas City tries to use the same tactics on our own homeless population. These are just a few of the programs we are aware of, and we are trying to come up with a plan to stop them.

The Teacher's Impact on My Life

As I sit here, one lesson that sticks out in my mind is Mark Victor Hansen telling me, "Richard, I'll help you as much as I can, as long as it doesn't interfere with my commitments."

I believe, in essence, what he was saying was that he would help me as much as possible, but at the same time, it was I who had to make my dreams about my organization a reality. He could tutor me and introduce me to his friends, but when it came to making things happen, I was the one who was responsible for my dreams.

Over the years, that's what he has done. He has literally introduced me to hundreds, if not thousands, of his friends. The majority of the people he's introduced me to I can now call my friends. Billionaires, millionaires, writers, speakers, producers, publishers, agents, movie stars, musicians, motivators—the list goes on and on. And still, after all these years, I know that he can introduce me to them, but if I need their help, it's up to me to do my own recruiting. And that's fine with me, because I have the fire in my belly. I have the vision and the compassion to see my dreams come true, and like I have said before, Mark taught me that billion-dollar word: "NEXT." When I need something or someone to help my mission go forward, I don't stop until I get what I want. If things don't work out one way, then I just try another, and so on and so on. A lot of times, I step out on what some would call blind faith. It may be blind to them, but to me it's an opportunity that has presented itself. For instance, my second trip to Los Angeles was for one of Mark's seminars. At that time, I wasn't that well-known, and I was still struggling to make ends meet. When Mark was in town, he had invited me to come to California and attend his seminar. I had told him that I couldn't because I didn't have the money to take the trip. I sort of thought he might give me the money to come, but that wasn't his reply. He looked over at me and said, "Well, Mr. Tripp, if you want to attend the seminar, you'll find a way."

To this day, I don't know if he was testing me or not, but by the time he got on the plane, I knew that one way or another, I was going to go to that seminar. I think he knew it too. For a few months, I saved money for that trip, because I had a gut feeling I was supposed to be there. I had a feeling that something would happen there that would make it worth whatever I had to do to get there.

The time approached for the trip. I had enough money to buy the airplane ticket, rent a car, and buy food. However, I didn't have enough money to get a hotel room. My plan was to stay in the rental car for three days. As I got on the plane, I remember thinking to myself, "Here I am, going to California. I have an event coming up next month. I should be out trying to make the money to pay for that, instead of taking this plane to Los Angeles so I can rent a car and live in it for three days."

I arrived at about twelve thirty in the early morning. I went and rented the car and headed for Riverside, California, which is where the seminar was being held. With all the traffic and after getting lost a couple times, it took me about four hours to get there. Knowing that the seminar didn't start until eight o'clock, I parked on the street, climbed in the back seat, and went to sleep for a few hours.

When I awoke, I went into the hotel where the seminar was being held, found their restroom, washed up, combed my hair, and then went hunting for the room where the seminar would be held. They had a reception desk in the hallway. I approached the woman manning the desk and said, "My name is Richard Tripp. Mark invited me." The woman behind the desk said, "Let me see if we have a badge with your name on it." She looked through the boxes of badges, looked up, and said, "Here it is, Mr. Tripp. Go over to that next table and they will give you a workbook for the seminar."

"Okay, thank you. Is Mark in the room?"

"No, he hasn't come down yet, but he'll be here shortly." I walked over to the table, got my workbook, and stood there watching people talk to each other in the hallway.

About that time, Mark walked down the hallway. People started running over to him to get their books autographed. He signed the books as I headed over toward him. He looked up and saw me. A big grin spread across his face, and he said, "Richard, you see I told you if you wanted to attend, you would find a way." Then he gave me a big bear hug and started introducing me to everyone that was there having their books signed. I felt like a star myself, telling them about the work I did and how I was in the Chicken Soup books. It sort of made me feel kind of special. Several people asked me if I would autograph the story that was written about me if they bought the book. I said, "Sure." I stood there and signed a few with Mark until he decided that it was time to go inside.

"By the way, Richard, I want you to sit up front," he said.

"Okay, Mark," I said.

Now, I had seen Mark speak at churches a few times, and I knew he could inspire people with his stories, but this seminar was a lot different than a church. To begin with, there were a couple of thousand people in this room, and it seemed to me that the more people for whom Mark performed, the better he got. He blew their socks off. He spoke for a couple of hours by himself, and then his partner, Jack Canfield, got on stage with him. Jack is a motivational speaker himself and co-author of *Chicken Soup for the Soul.* Let me tell you, when you get the two of them together on stage, you truly get motivated. After they finished, we went into the morning break. After the break, Mark got back up on stage and told the audience that he had someone special there who he wanted them to meet. He looked at me and said, "Richard, would you come up here a minute, please?"

I was surprised when he called me up on that stage and started explaining to the audience who I was and how he had met me and all about the work I did with the poor and homeless in Kansas City. He told them the whole story as I stood there, and then he said, "Richard, would you like to say something to the audience?"

Standing there, I felt like my legs were made of rubber, and I know I must have turned a bunch of different reddish colors when he handed me the mic. I started speaking about the next event I had coming up and why I did the events in the way I did them. When I was finished speaking, I headed back to my seat. As I started down the steps, I received a standing ovation from the entire audience. As I made my way back to my seat, people shook my hand and gave me hugs. They took my picture and asked me for my card so they could get in touch with me after the seminar. When I got back to my seat, the guy that I was sitting next to asked me if I would like to have lunch with him and his wife at the break. I accepted. When lunch rolled around, the guy and his wife asked me to sit at their table. At Mark's seminars, lunch is provided for the attendees. As we sat there talking, the guy asked me for my room number. He wanted to get together later that night and compare notes about the seminar. I was a little embarrassed, but I told him I didn't have a room.

"Well, where are you staying?" he asked.

"Well, to tell you the truth, I didn't have the money to rent a room at these prices."

"Well, where are you going to stay during the seminar," he asked.

"To tell the truth, I have a rented car parked down the street. I was going stay in it," I replied.

He said, "Mr. Tripp, I tell you what, I'll rent you a room. All you have to do is send me a receipt, and I can hold it on my taxes. Is that okay with you?"

"That's fine with me. Are you sure I won't be putting you out?"

"Nope, as long as you send me the receipt for my taxes, it will be a donation to your cause."

I thanked him, and he rented me a room for the three days of the seminar. That was my second surprise of the day. The third one would knock my socks off.

At the last session of the day, Mark got up on stage and asked one of the servers to bring him an empty pitcher. When he got it, he said, "People, let's take up a collection for Richard Tripp and Care of Poor People." He took a one hundred dollar bill out of his pocket, put it in the pitcher, and started passing it around the room. I don't remember how much was collected, but I do remember that it was enough to pay for my next event. The moral of this story is simple: when that little voice starts speaking to me and I get the feeling to step out on blind faith and do something or go somewhere, it usually benefits me.

These days, I try to attend all of Mark's seminars, and I urge you, if you want to pursue a career in writing, speaking, or networking, to do the same. Mark brings together the best in their fields to teach you the ins and outs of the career field you want to pursue. One of the main reasons I go to the seminars is for the benefits I get from networking. One thing I learned from my first seminar was, if you want to be the best in whatever your field is, why not surround yourself with the best? If you want to be a millionaire, would it make more sense to hang out with other millionaires, or with someone who hasn't made their first million? The answer: hang out with the millionaires. Why? Because you just might learn something from them that will help make you a millionaire. They have already achieved what you want, which means they might be able to give you the advice you need to achieve your goals. They have already faced the roadblocks you might come up against, and it will give you an edge if you know what to expect. You can be ready for it. The same holds true for any goal. You should surround yourself with those who have the same goals. I know that I personally I have achieved a lot of my goals because of the networking I've done and the contacts I've made at Mark's seminars. Not only have I made good contacts, but also lifetime friends I would have never made or met any other way.

Well, my plane is here. It's time to step out on blind faith again and take this manuscript to the seminar.

Helpers along the Way

Just like Jesus Christ had helpers along the way to help him with his mission on earth, I have been blessed with helpers to make my mission of helping America's poor and homeless brothers' and sisters' lives easier. In this chapter, I'm going to mention just a few of those who have helped me make COPP the organization it is today. While I can't mention them all, or how we got together, I'll mention a few.

I'll start with Charley Green. When I'm feeling down and depressed, the first person I call to inspire me—is Charley. We have become very good friends over the years. I first talked to Charley when he phoned me years ago. At the time, he was a janitor at Unity Church of Overland Park, but on the side he was a wannabe writer and speaker. Today, I can say he's made his dream come true. He has written several books and also is starting to work as a speaker for a living. He's come a long way from the janitor job. He was also a good friend of Mark Victor Hansen. Mark told Charley to contact me and help me if he could. At the time, he was selling vitamins in one of the ventures he and Mark were doing. He called me to see if I would like to get involved in the business.

He invited me to his house to listen to a sales meeting one night. I went and listened, but told him it just wasn't something I wanted to do. We still became friends. I could tell him what I thought about things going on in my life. I shared storied about COPP, and he gave constructive ideas on how he thought I should precede with my ideas.

While it was my choice to make the final decision on how to proceed, it was good to have a sounding board. Today, I can say a lot of COPP ideas were bounced off Charley before a decision was made to proceed or scrap them.

In some ways, the people I'm telling you about, although they are good friends, have become more like family over the years. Calling them helpers isn't enough. Without them, COPP would not have had the impact it's had in our city or around the country. Thanks to all the media exposure I've had, I have been blessed at times to get calls from people who have heard me speak about my goals and want to help me make them happen.

A couple of such volunteers were Gary G. and Chuck D. Their last names are abbreviated because neither of them would appreciate the publicity, though I assure you they both deserve recognition, and Care of Poor People could not have become the household name it is in Kansas City, Missouri, without their unselfish volunteering. These men not only gave of their time but also of their resources. A lot of the funding we received in the early years was because they dug into their own pockets and came up with cash. As a matter of fact, Chuck D. believed in what I was doing so much that he went out and bought me clothes and shoes. He also paid for lodging and airfare so I could travel around the country and raise the funds I would need to help maintain COPP's budget in the early years.

It all started when Chuck D. heard me speaking on the radio one Sunday and told Gary G. about what I was trying to do. Chuck D. owned a communications company, and Gary G. worked for him. Both men decided to get involved, and the rest is history. I still speak to them once in a while. They'll call me and ask me how things are going, and I know if I need them, all I have to do is give them a call. (A side note: At one of the events Chuck and Gary were organizing with me, Chuck brought a volunteer, a women he had been dating, to help us. During the event he asked her to marry him. She accepted, and several weeks later they were married. That was about eight years ago. They are still a happy couple.)

One day several years ago, I walked out the front door of my house one morning and the taxicab I'd been leasing was gone. It had been stolen from right in front of my house. To say the least, I was frantic. That taxi was my bread and butter. I didn't know what I was going do. I called Gary and told him what had happened. There was a moment of silence on the other end, and Gary finally said, "Well, Tripp, I wouldn't get over concerned. It will probably show up."

I thought to myself, "That's easy for you to say."

He must have heard my thoughts, because the next thing he said was, "Richard, I know it's probably hard for you to believe it now, but it will work out. Maybe God has got some other plans for you. You know anytime anything has happened to me, God has always had something better waiting down the line."

I said, "All right, Gary, I'll let you go for now. I've got some other calls to make." After I hung up the phone, I sat there thinking. Was he right? I'm afraid his faith was bigger than mine at that moment. All I could see was disaster. How would I pay the bills without that taxi? How would I have money to run COPP?

There must have been a million thoughts running around in my mind, and none of them had a blessing behind it.

That story brings me to my next special helper, the Reverend Nancy Jerome of Unity Church of Overland Park. The first time I saw Nancy was when she was serving lunch to Mark Victor Hansen the day he had appeared at Unity so many years ago. Back then, she was the church's associate pastor. Over the years, we have become very good friends. I might add that she is one of the very few advisers I not only listen to, but also actively seek advice from. She advises me on different matters that affect COPP, and she provides advice about our activities. I feel she is a woman with great knowledge who is well connected in our community. She's a true asset, not only to her church, but also to the community itself. She has been a special asset to COPP and to me personally.

After I'd gotten off the phone with Gary G., I called Nancy to tell her that my taxi had been stolen. I also told her a part of the story I hadn't shared with Gary. I told her that when the thieves had taken my taxi, they had killed my dogs with some type of poison. I guess they did that to keep them quiet. That's the only explanation I've ever been able to come up with. You see, I live in a Kansas City ghetto. COPP needed a place to store its materials, and a house was donated. We use the building as a warehouse, but it is in the worst part of the city. I knew that when I moved in, but out of necessity for space, I did it anyway. I never thought someone would kill the dogs I used to guard the place.

I told her my story and she said, "Richard, I'm sure sorry to hear that. I sure hope they find your taxi."

"Me too," I replied. "If they don't, I don't know what I'll do."

She said, "We'll be praying for you at church, Richard."

I thanked her, hung up the phone, and went on about my daily routine. At least I did what I could without my car. For three days I sat in that house and only left to walk to the store. The police hadn't found my taxi, so I didn't have any way to make a living.

On Friday I got a call from Nancy. She asked me how things were going and if I was coming to church on Sunday. I told her that my situation hadn't changed and that I would not be able to make it to church because I didn't have any wheels. We talked for a while before she said she had to go. I didn't really give the call a second thought. I just thought she was concerned about my welfare.

I sat at the house all weekend. On Monday morning I decided to walk to the store to buy cigarettes with my last bit of change. When I returned home, there was a big manila envelope sitting by the door. It had Unity Church of Overland Park printed on it. I picked it up, took it inside, laid it on my bed, and went to the kitchen for a cup of coffee. I figured it was a magazine or something the mailman had brought.

As I reentered the room, the package caught my eye. I picked it up, and when I opened it, I got the shock of my life. Nancy had told the head minister at the church about my troubles. The head minister had told the church, and the congregation had taken up a collection on Sunday to help me out. The note in the envelope read, "Dear Mr. Tripp, this money is not to be used for COPP, but rather it is given to you to buy a car you can use to make a living. You have given to the community, and now it's time for us, the members of Unity Church of Overland Park, to help you in your time of need."

In that envelope were all kinds of twenty-dollar bills and checks. The contents totaled more than six thousand dollars. I sat there for a while, just looking at the checks and cash, almost not believing what I was seeing. After I quit crying, I called Nancy and told her to thank the people who had donated the money. I told her that a friend was on his way to pick me up and we were going shop for a car that I could use as a taxi. And that's what I did. The taxi I drive today is because of the love and compassion the members of Unity Church of Overland Park had for me in my time of need.

Another helper, who has been there almost since I organized that first Christmas Breakfast for the Homeless, is Dr. Jarvis Williams, a guy we've lovingly nicknamed "Skip Town" because he travels more than anyone I've ever met. Over the years he has done a lot for us. More than once he's paid for the food we've served to the poor and homeless. He's let us use his parking lot. He's allowed us to collect and hand out donated materials on his property. He's even paid the taxes on the COPP house. All I ever have to do is let him know we are in need, and he will figure out a way to help us.

These next helpers are a few of my Jewish brothers. I met them when I gave a speech at a Jewish temple. Their names are John I. and Michael S. These two gentlemen have been helping me for the past several years. They are the reason COPP is a household word in many Jewish homes in Kansas City. At the time I gave that speech at that temple, I had no place to hold my events. If an event was on the horizon, I would have to find a building, find park space, or throw a block party. When John heard of my need for a building, he and Michael started speaking to developers in the Kansas City area. One of the members of their temple, Tom Levitt, came through for COPP in a big way. Mr. Levitt donates the use of a warehouse to COPP twice a year so we can hold our events. Needless to say, we could not afford to rent the warehouse. Tom takes his generosity one step further. He not only donates use of the building, he also pays the city for all the permits we need to hold an event at his warehouse.

I hope this chapter has shown you that while I have been the driving force in realizing my dream of helping those who are down and out, I have not been the only one working to make it happen. Making the dream a reality required much assistance from special members of the community. The special people spoken about here are joined by hundreds of others, as well as many Kansas City churches and temples. They have blessed my efforts, and they helped make COPP a household name here in Kansas City and the across the country.

The Price I've Paid

When I started COPP years ago, I could not have known how far the organization would come, how many people would count on the decisions I have to make, or just how much of an effect I could have on my community. I don't take that responsibility lightly. As a matter of fact, it's never far from my thoughts. Today, just about anywhere I go in my town, I'm recognized by the public as pseudo-celebrity. That means I have to carry a certain image in everything I do. There are still those who would like to have something they could use to discredit me and bring the end to my organization. The truth is that we're too good at what we do and how we do it. We are able to accomplish with thousands of dollars what it takes the others millions of dollars to do. I'm convinced the difference is that we're able to motivate the public. We don't just motivate the public to send funds. We are also able to get them to come down, do the work, and see where the funds and materials really go. We don't have a lot of overhead, because most of the work is done by volunteers.

I guess the place I've paid the highest price over the years is with my family. Although they are all proud of the difference I've been able to make for those hurting, my family life hasn't been that great. There have been times that members of my own family—mother, brothers, and sisters—have said to me, "Rick, we want you to come down and spend some time with us, but please leave COPP at home. All you ever talk about is COPP." On another occasion, one of my daughters said to me, "Dad, I want my dad to spend the weekend with me; I don't want 'the legend' Richard Tripp; I want my dad Richard Tripp." When one of your own children says something like that, it can have a lasting effect and make you rethink your priorities.

I've tried to let all my children know that I'll be there for them if they need me. I've told them that I am their father first, but at the same time I have a responsibility to those that put their trust in me on the street. I am as committed to the well-being of those poor and homeless brothers and sisters now, as I was when I started COPP all those years ago.

In 2004, we had a board meeting one night as we prepared for one of our survival events. As I drove to the meeting, I got to feeling ill. When I arrived, the other members were already present. I told them to go on to the meeting and let me know how things went. I was going to go home and go to bed. I thought I might have a bout of the flu or something. I was so weak I could hardly move. I didn't really know what was wrong, but I knew something wasn't right.

One of the board members said, "Hey, Tripp, you want us to take you to the doctor or something?"

"No, guys, go on and have the meeting. I'll make it home okay," I said as I drove off. I made it home, made it out of the car, got into my bedroom, and lay down before I passed out.

The next morning I woke up and felt something wet under the blankets. I reached down and got the shock of my life when I pulled my hand out from under the covers. It was covered in blood. I knew I was in trouble. I called 911, asked them to send an ambulance to my address, and explained what was wrong. The next thing I did was call my mother to tell her where the paramedics would be taking me. I yelled to the homeless guy I had staying with me, woke him up, and told him to help me get dressed and out to the front yard where I could meet the ambulance.

He helped me make it to the front steps, where I sat down and waited for the ambulance. The fire department showed up first, and a couple of firefighters started towards me. I hadn't thought about my dog, who was on a chain in the front yard. He started for the firefighters and just about got one of them.

One of the firefighters said to the other, "Get an axe. Let's put him down."

"No," I yelled. "Danny, get this damn dog." Then I yelled at the firefighters, "Don't hurt that dog."

Danny grabbed the dog just as the ambulance arrived. The firefighters got me on a stretcher. They started taking my blood pressure, and they tried to put an IV in my arm. They continued to try to put an IV in me all the way to the hospital. They never did get one to work. My blood pressure was just about as low as it could go, and I was starting to go into shock. I had lost a considerable amount of blood. By the time they got me to the hospital, I felt like I was reliving the nightmare of the events that had happened years earlier. The first thing they had to do was put a central line in my neck for the IV. Then they had to run the tube down my nose again. This time I sort of knew what was going on, so I tried to relax more than I had the first time. They put something in the IV to put me out. While I was out, they did a scope.

When I awoke, the tube was out of my nose, blood was being given to me via the IV, and I was in a room. The doctor came in and said, "Mr. Tripp, do you know where you are?"

I said, "I think at Truman Hospital."

He said, "That's right. You seem to have a bleed. We did a scope but didn't find it, so we're going to give you blood for a while, and maybe tomorrow or the next day we'll do another scope on you and fix the leak."

"Doc, how long will I be here?"

"Well, we're not sure, Mr. Tripp. Maybe a week or so."

"But I can't afford to be here that long, Doc. I've got an event coming up next month and bills to pay."

He said, "Well, Mr. Tripp, until we can get the bleeding to stop, you'll be with us."

He left the room, and I lay there thinking, "What in the hell am I going do?" I couldn't help but wonder what was going to happen to COPP if I died. Who would make the events work? I knew I had good people working on my board, but what I was worried about was whether I had taught them enough to be able to handle any problems that might arise at an event. That's what was on my mind as I went to sleep.

When I awoke, my mother and father were there. She asked me how I was feeling.

I said, "Mom, it's just like the last time … the central lines and everything. They're saying they haven't been able to get the bleeding to stop, and they're going to have to put a lot of pints of blood in me."

"Well, don't worry about it, Son. They have plenty of blood."

"I know it, Mom. Don't tell anybody, but right now, I don't know if it's the blood loss or what, but I'm scared."

"I know, Son, but they'll get the blood loss stopped eventually."

"Have you talked to Dawn?"

"She's supposed to be on her way up here with Ricky, Christy, and Danny. Jody is supposed to be on her way too." For those wondering my oldest son Keith has made some bad mistakes in his life and has been a resident of the State of Missouri prison system for quite some time.

"Mom, I need you to make a call."

"Okay, who to?"

"I need you to call John I. Tell him what's going on. He'll let the rest of the board members know I'm here. Tell him I need to speak to him."

"Okay, Son, I'll give him a call."

"Okay, Mom," I said just before I fell asleep. When I awoke, the nurse was checking my IV. She said, "Mr. Tripp, you have some visitors in the waiting room. Would you like me to send them in?"

"Yes, please."

In walks John I. and some of the other COPP board members—Michael S., Scott Z., and his wife Kim Z. I was glad to see them all.

"How you doing, Tripp?" someone asked.

"Oh, I guess as good as can be expected," I said.

Kim said, "I knew something was really wrong with you when you didn't come upstairs for the board meeting."

"Well, I didn't want to worry you guys."

We chitchatted for a while, and they tried to convince me that the upcoming event would be great even if I weren't there.

And then Kim Z spoke up and said, "Don't worry about the event. We'll make sure it goes on okay. You just worry about getting well and getting out of here."

I thanked them for coming, and as they readied to leave, I asked John I. if I could speak to him privately.

"Sure," he said. The others left the room, and I looked up at John and said, "Hey, Bro, I'm worried that I might not make it out of this hospital this time. Just in case I'm right, I want your promise to keep the COPP program and the events up and running. I know it's a lot to ask, but you're the only one I *know* can make it happen."

"Don't worry, Brother, I'll keep COPP going if anything happens to you."

About that time the door opened and in walked my kids—Dawn, Chris, Danny, Ricky, and Jody. Although John already knew some of them, I introduced him to everyone.

After they'd all exchanged pleasantries, John said, "I'm going to get going now. I'll come see you later, Tripp."

"Okay, John, thank you for coming." As he left, I was feeling better. I now had John's word that if something did go wrong, he would keep COPP running. It was nice being surrounded by the majority of my children in that hospital room. Combine that with the relief I experienced in knowing I'd hand-picked my successor, and I sort of relaxed a little.

There are not many people in this world whose word I trust, but my bro John I. is a man of integrity. When he gives you his word, it's as good as money in the bank.

I ended up staying in that hospital room for a week or so. Each day I expected the bleeding to stop, and each day that failed to happen. I was scared. They did finally get it to stop, but by then I was a basket case. I had just known for sure that I was a goner. I wondered how much blood they would they give me before they decided that it wasn't going to help. Lying in that hospital bed, bleeding as heavily as I was, and my mind started playing games with me.

On about the third day of my stay, my stepmother and my half brothers from my dad's second marriage paid me a visit. That was a special visit, because they lived a few hundred miles away. I was raised mostly by my father and stepmother from the time I was about ten or so. My half brother Randy was about five when I moved into my father's house. One might say I watched him grow up and protected him from the bullies at school. We had been really close. I was really surprised by this visit, because I knew that Randy had been sick himself for some time. He'd been having problems with his legs and could barely walk, but even with his problems, he was there for his big brother. As they left that day, he looked in my eyes and said, "I love you, Bro. Hurry up and get out of here." He bent over, put a kiss on my forehead, and said, "I'll see you when you get out of here, Bro."

In addition to my family members, many members of the clergy stopped by to check on me, and a lot of radio-station announcers with whom I'd done community programming shows also stopped by.

I had a lot of different people from many different faiths praying for my recovery, and it was comforting knowing that they all cared.

The day arrived when I was finally leaving the hospital. The doctors had gotten the bleeding to stop. They determined that my arthritis medication had started the bleed. I checked out of the hospital, headed home, got in my car, and headed for my mother's house to stay for the weekend.

Of course, I spent most of that weekend on her computer sending out e-mails about COPP's next event. By then it was only a few weeks away. For the next few weeks, I recuperated from that hospital stay and worked on the Survival V Event for the homeless.

I had just about recuperated from that stay when I received a phone call that would eventually have me making the hardest decision I've ever made in regard to a COPP event. The call came from my sister, Pam. She said Randy had been taken to the hospital in Bolivar, Missouri, by ambulance; he couldn't even walk. I dropped everything I was doing and drove to Bolivar to find out how he was doing.

By the time I got there, Randy was in intensive care. I had to wait with some other family members until it was my turn to go in and see him. They were only allowing each family member a few minutes to talk with him. When I got to his room, it looked like he had gained a hundred pounds. He was so pale; his skin tone resembled the sheets on his bed. He looked over, saw me, and smiled. I said, "Hey, Bro, there's something wrong with this picture. I'm supposed to be the only one in the hospital receiving visitors."

He said, "Well, believe me, I don't want to be here."

"How are you feeling?" I asked.

"How do I look?" was his reply.

"Not good, but that's beside the point. What do the doctors say, anyway?"

He stared at me for a second, and then he said, "They say I'm dying, Rick."

From the look on his face, I could tell he was being serious. "Well, what do they say is wrong with you?"

"They're running tests, but they think it's leukemia."

"Can't they give you a transplant or something?"

"I don't know."

"Well, Randy, I'll be the first in line to let them test my bone marrow. Maybe I'll be a match. I mean I don't know that much about what would make a match of the marrow, but we have the same father, so it might match."

"Thanks, Bro, but I don't think it will do much good, even with a transplant," he said. "I really feel like my time is just about up. Speaking of time, Rick, aren't you getting ready to do your event this coming week?"

"Well, since you mentioned it, yep, it's next Saturday."

"You should be up there getting ready, instead of here at this hospital, Bro."

"Well, my little brother is more important," I replied.

"Nonsense, Rick. You know what you do is important, and besides, you can call me on the phone to find out how I'm doing."

"You sure you don't want me to rent a motel room in town and stay here with you for the rest of the week, Randy?"

"Nope, I want you to be up there doing the work you're supposed to be doing." About that time my stepmother and one of my half sisters walked in and started talking to Randy. He looked over at me and said, "Call me tomorrow, Rick."

I said my good-byes to the rest of the family, walked over, and gave my brother a kiss on his forehead just liked he'd done to me a few weeks earlier.

I left and headed back to Kansas City to get everything ready for the Survival V Event. Driving back to Kansas City, I did a lot of daydreaming about our childhood. I just had a feeling that he wasn't coming out of that hospital. I tried to shake it off, but it just wouldn't leave.

When I got back to Kansas City, there were plenty of last-minute event details to tend to. I talked to my brother on the phone every day. About four days before the Survival V Event was to begin, I was talking to my brother when he suddenly said, "Rick, I can't get my breath."

"Well, put the phone down and call your nurse," I told him.

The last words I heard my brother say were, "I can't breathe, I can't breathe, Rick."

I hung up the phone, redialed the hospital, and told them what my brother had just told me. I told them to get a nurse in his room to check on him. I also told them to have my sister give me a call when she got there, so I would know if I should drop everything and head back down there. I then called Dawn and told her to go to the hospital and keep me informed on how Randy was doing. My sister called me a few hours later and told me that Randy had gone into a coma. They didn't know how long he might be in it.

I was trying to get things laid out for the event and was planning to go visit my brother the next evening, the day before Thanksgiving. But that morning, Dawn called and said, "Dad, Uncle Randy just died." I told her I would be down there that night. I was heartbroken, but there wasn't anything I could really do. I drove down that night, but they had already moved his body to the funeral home. I wouldn't be able to see him until after Thanksgiving.

I assumed the funeral would be sometime Friday, but it didn't turn out that way. For some reason, the funeral home decided the funeral would be Saturday at noon instead of Friday afternoon. And with their decision, I had to make a decision, probably the hardest one I've ever had to make my whole life. I was going to have to either go to my COPP event—an event that I'd been planning for a year, an event that I had worried about even when I was lying in the hospital—or go to my brother's funeral and leave the event in the hands of the board members.

There were pros and cons for each option, and I felt that I would be criticized for whichever option I chose. If something went wrong at the event because I wasn't there, if there was trouble and my team couldn't handle it, I would be criticized for not being there to take care of things. However, if I wasn't at my brother's funeral, I would have family members expressing their views on my not being there. They would say that my event meant more than my half brother. They'd say that I didn't love him. Either way I went, I was up a creek without a paddle. I spent Thanksgiving with my kids in Springfield. All day long I pondered the decision before me.

That evening I made my decision. I called my stepmother's house and told her I couldn't take the chance of missing the event. I told her that if something went wrong or if my team couldn't handle a situation, then everything I had worked for could be jeopardized. I said, "I hope you understand, Mom. You know I loved Randy with all my heart, but I think he would want me to do the event if he was alive, so that's what I'm going do."

The next morning I started for Kansas City but made a detour to see my brother at the funeral home. It was hard for me to view his body lying there motionless. I noticed that he was wearing the shirt I bought him to go to one of my speaking engagements the year before. I had also bought a matching shirt for myself. I know it might sound like I'm nuts, but I think that was an omen to go ahead and do the event. It had been a hard decision for me, but sometimes in life you have to make them. And sometimes, even in the hard decisions you make, there are silver linings. Because I skipped the funeral, I was able to attend the event and dedicate it in Randy's honor. The dedication was front-page news that Sunday in the *Kansas City Star*. People, who'd never met Randy Bruce Tripp, knew he had existed in this world, thanks to his big brother's involvement in the Survival V Event for Kansas City's poor and homeless.

These are just a few of examples of the price I have paid over the years in order to help the poor and homeless in Kansas City.

Where I Stand Today and What Are My Hopes for Tomorrow

I started what has become COPP when I was forty-three years old. Today I am fifty-nine; that makes COPP sixteen years old. That's hard for me to believe. It seems like I started it yesterday. I sometimes ask myself, "Where did all those years and experiences go?" It's been fourteen years since I last held a half pint of Canadian Mist in my hand, let alone downed it in a single drink.

I have outlived a lot of the people I mentioned in this book.

I guess you could say I'm approaching the winter of my life, and the question I ask myself right now is, "Have I done enough?"

The answer is no. It will always be no, so long as there are human beings being hurt by the systems that are in place to help them. I must admit, I'm tired and feeling my age, but I have not seen any reason to stop fighting the good fight. If I need a reason to continue doing what I'm doing, there are plenty. Each time I see one of my brothers or sisters being mistreated, lying on a sidewalk, sleeping under a bridge, or eating from a dumpster in an alley, I have a reason to fight. As I watch all the affordable housing units in my city being torn down so they can put in condos, I have a reason to fight.

I'm disgusted when I see those who are down and out being turned away from a gas station where they are trying to get water in a jug to survive. I think to myself that those doing the denying would gladly give water to a stray dog, yet they turn the human away.

When I see people throwing away food at restaurants and stores instead of feeding those who are hungry, I ask myself, "I wonder what those same people doing those things would do if, God forbid, the situation was reversed and they were the ones needing help."

When I see hospitals and libraries kicking those who are already down out into the cold, then I know why I keep doing what I do. I am also aware that I have yet to scratch the surface in my effort to alleviate the nightmarish lives some of my brothers and sisters face on the streets of our nation. I know that I don't have a lot of the answers, but God has given me the gifts of motivation, love, and compassion so I can make a difference. I try to motivate those who do have the answers; I try to get involved and solve problems, rather than ignore them.

The problems that the homeless face are very complex; solving them won't be easy. But I have faith in America, and I believe that these problems can be remedied. There are solutions to problems such as unemployment, lack of low-income housing, and nonexistent health insurance, but in order to solve these problems we must first *try* to solve these problems. If you don't try, then you've already failed.

COPP is no longer an idea; it's a reality. The organization has become one of Kansas City's most talked-about organizations. We are not only known for the work we do here in our community, but also for the work Richard Tripp inspires around the globe. Our board of directors is made up of a group of top business leaders from our community. They are joined by a team of caring committee members and an army of community volunteers. These people working together are able to make changes in the way the homeless are treated in our community, and they save lives at the same time. I'm proud of the team I have been able to pull together from my community, because just like me, they are all volunteers. That means that all the money that's donated to COPP goes directly into the programs. Today, thanks to them, I have opportunities to pursue other goals. The board, the committees, and the volunteers are able to take care of our two major annual events, Spring Break and the Survival Events, while I focus my energies on starting and expanding new COPP programs, locally, nationally, and globally.

These days, I travel a lot spreading the word and participating in speaking engagements all across our nation. I attempt to motivate others to get involved with the homeless in their communities by telling true stories about where I started and how far I've come. I show people that no matter where they start, they can make a difference in our world for those who are hurting. If you would like to invite me to speak to your community, tell my stories, and motivate those around you who would like to make a difference, I can be reached through our Web site, www.coppinc.com, or you can call me at 816-483-4081.

Epilogue

I'm sitting here at Kansas City International waiting for a plane to take me to Los Angeles for the Mark Victor Hansen Mega Book Seminar. I'm thinking about the future of this book and my career. I've tried to show the readers some of my life stories. Yet I still have plenty to tell, and I know there will be other opportunities coming my way to expand on those story lines. I guess the difference in my writing this book or letting another author write it is simple enough: I personally lived the stories I've written about.

None of us knows what will happen in the future, but just like others, I have my hopes and dreams. I believe my life story may inspire people to follow my lead and opt to make a difference in their own communities. Whether Christian, Jew, Muslim, Hindu, or a member of any other religion, we are told to love our God first and then to show his love to our brothers and sisters by treating them as we would ourselves. For every loving act you do for those in need, it will be given back to you tenfold by our father in heaven.

I, as any other human being, have questions about life. I would like to know why God has blessed me with the opportunities I've been blessed with to make life better for those who are hurting. Although I don't have all the answers, I think back to all the things that have happened to me that bring me to the point of writing this book. I recognize that God has even used my mistakes to propel me in the direction of making changes for those who are hurting the most. If I would have listened to or followed God's law in the first place, I wouldn't have had to live the life I now live. At the same time, it is amazing to me that even though I made those mistakes God has continued to bless me. And it is written, "All things work together for the good of those who love God."

Please underestimate me, but never underestimate God, for with him all things are possible. My life proves it. I don't know where his love and blessings will lead me in the future or what problems or obstacles I'll have to face, but I can tell you this, with his help I'll keep up the good fight for those who are hurting.

I thank God every day for opening my eyes and my heart to the plight of the poor and homeless and for giving me a mission in life. I also thank him for lead-ing me down the path that led me to some of my mentors: Mark Victor Hansen, Joe Tye, Chip Collins, and Charley Green. Throughout the years, I have gained knowledge from each of them. They help me keep my mission going forward, and I know I couldn't have had the effect I have had helping those who are down-and-out without the lessons I've learned from them and other special teachers along the way.

From the day I first picked Mark up in my cab, life has become a learning experience. I have been blessed to be on stage with a number of the top marketers in the world; I have met the top speakers in the world; and I have learned some of their secrets. The first thing I learned was that in order to reach people in marketing, you have to have a passion for what you are doing. It can't be faked; people will see right through it. There has to be a fire in your belly when you're explaining yourself to the public. Keep in mind that number one rule: "never fear, never quit." Don't start doubting yourself because of some negative comment someone might make. Go with the feeling in your belly; be real and true to yourself. Just remember that the majority of the leaders today have been told "no" by someone at one time or another. That rejection likely helped inspire them to become the leader they are today. It's simple. They didn't give up on their dreams. It doesn't matter what their dream was. What matters is that all dreams have the potential to come true. Remember, the word *next* is a winner.

Another thing I have learned is that it's important to treat everyone with respect; take time to listen to people. I know several people I've met over the years who made me feel like I was number one, regardless of what they may have really thought of my ideas. The point is that while I was in their company, they had a way of making me think I was the most important thing in their life.

Mark is good at the art of listening. So was a beloved friend that just died, John Jordan Buck O'Neil, the founder of the Negro league here in Kansas City. With all the negativity he had to face in his life because of the color of his skin, you would think he would be bitter. But not Buck. When you were in his company he made you think you were the most important person alive. Although I believe this skill comes from the heart, it's still an art. Practice it. It will help you in whatever you face in life. In other words, take the time to let others know you care about them and their problems. Tell them why you feel you're blessed to be with them. Let them know they count. In a sense, help them turn life's lemons into lemonade. Every morning when you get up, expect a miracle, no matter how bad things look.

My hopes for this book, *Please Underestimate Me,* are many. First, I would like it to be a number one book, but more importantly, I would like the book's message to be spread. That message is simple: love our brothers and sisters on the streets of America as we love ourselves.

I hope this book gives people a view into some of the problems the poor and homeless of America face. I then hope it gives people the courage to take on the systems that be and make a true difference for those hurting in their own communities. I also hope this book motivates the general public to check out the various poor and homeless programs in their hometown, and if something isn't right, I hope it motivates the public to fight the good fight and make it right, regardless of who or what retaliation they may face from the systems that be. I hope my book teaches you that regardless of who you are or where you are in life, you can make a difference. It only takes you getting involved in your community to make a change in the way people are treated. And finally, after reading my story, I hope you are aware that it wasn't really Richard G. Tripp changing the world, but rather the holy spirit of our Father in heaven changing my heart.

978-0-595-44210-2
0-595-44210-2

Printed in the United States
94333LV00003B/103-174/A

9 780595 442102